THE PACKAGE HOLIDAY

1968–1985

JAKE CLARK

Photography by

TREVOR CLARK

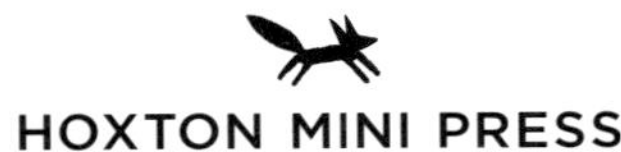

HOXTON MINI PRESS

ABOUT HOXTON MINI PRESS

Hello. Hoxton Mini Press is a small publisher from east London. We want to bring unusual photography to a wide audience; arty books should be beautiful (but they needn't be big or expensive). Books are no longer just about information. They are objects in their own right: things to collect and own and inspire. Thank you for supporting us.

www.hoxtonminipress.com

VINTAGE BRITAIN

A series celebrating the recent history of
these isles through rather nice photography.

BOOK ONE
The East End in Colour
1960–1980

BOOK TWO
The Isle of Dogs

BOOK THREE
Dog Show 1961–1978

BOOK FOUR
Paradise Street

BOOK FIVE
The East End in Colour
1980–1990

BOOK SIX
London Underground
1970–1980

BOOK SEVEN
Hackney Archive

BOOK EIGHT
Butlin's Holiday Camp 1982

BOOK NINE
London 1977–1987

BOOK TEN
London in the Snow

BOOK ELEVEN
A Very British Picnic

BOOK TWELVE
The London Pub

BOOK THIRTEEN
The National Health Service

BOOK FOURTEEN
The Package Holiday
1968–1985

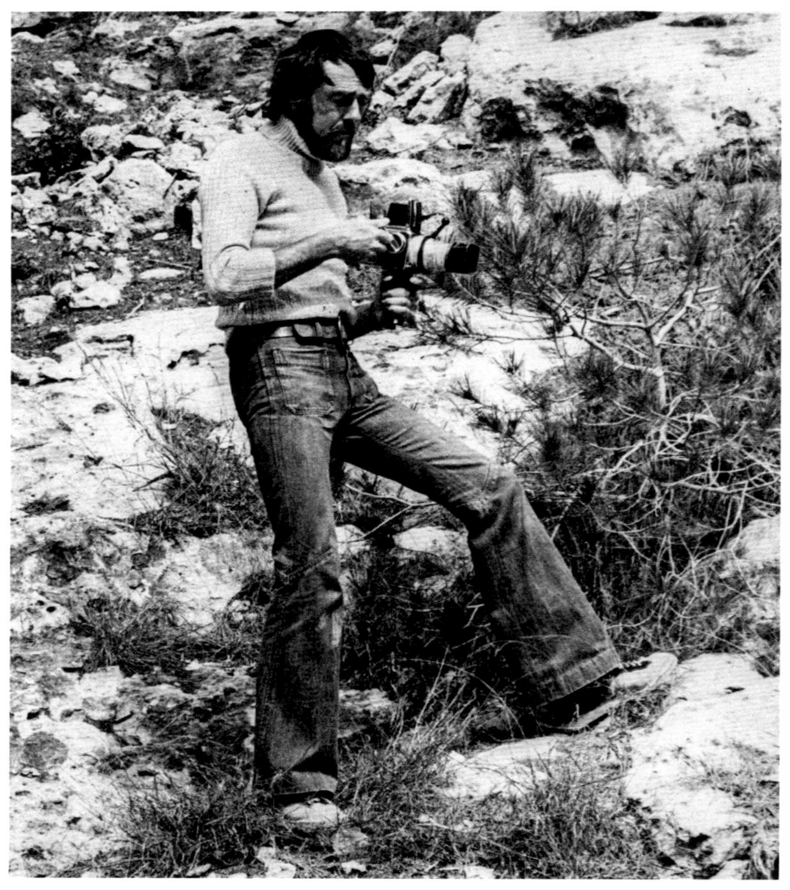

The British photographer Trevor Clark in Mallorca, c.1975.

TECHNICOLOUR TRAVEL

Selling a Mediterranean package holiday to the British in the 1970s meant overcoming three fears: foreign food, foreigners and flying. The first was easily managed, as tour operators quickly realised they could serve any local fare so long as it came with chips. Dealing with the average British tourist's mid-century mix of island-mentality xenophobia, cultural shyness and linguistic limitation, on the other hand, meant ensuring that the holiday was an organised, mass experience that precluded any need to interact with locals or go it alone. In-country necessities and activities were all catered for – whether a glass-bottomed boat trip or a group beach barbecue. And as for flying, Gatwick and Luton had become hubs for affordable charter airlines like Dan-Air, Britannia and Monarch which, with their fresh fleets of US-built Boeings, allayed safety worries while offering swish, new-world comfort.

Over the 1960s, UK foreign travel soared and the annual number of British tourists doubled to 5 million, turning package holiday operators into household names as Thomas Cook, whose elite 'Cook's Tours' in the 1870s presaged mass tourism's stratospheric 20th-century rise, was joined by Horizon, Clarksons, Intasun and Thomson. Things really took off when Provision One (a policy which prohibited operators from selling package holidays for less than the cost of a standard return flight) was repealed in 1971, sparking a massive price war. Operators began to offer a fortnight's all-inclusive beach break in Spain for around £76 per person (half a month's average wage) – a deal so affordable that the UK's old 'bucket-and-spade' seaside holiday camps could only watch as their visitor numbers dwindled. As Harry Goodman, the larger-than-life boss of Intasun, recalled decades later, 'It was cowboy country, like the beginning of the gold rush.'

By 1972, over a third of all British tourists holidayed in Spain. Photographer Trevor Clark, whose archive of brochure shoots of tour operators you see here, cannily foresaw this explosion in travel and moved to Mallorca in 1968 to set up a commercial studio after winding down his former premises in Soho. The Barking-born son of a door-to-door salesman, Clark learned camera skills during his RAF National Service and spent years after globetrotting as a photographer on luxury cruise ships. This exposure to sun and sea seemed to engender not just a professional but existential relationship to light, which perhaps explains his decision to emigrate to Portals Nous. A small and tranquil fishing village south of Palma, it was yet spared the effects of burgeoning hotel development occurring further down the coast in Magaluf, Santa Ponsa and Palma Nova.

Clark arrived at the tail end of Franco's dictatorship, not long after the 25th anniversary of the Spanish Civil War. Spain was spared of Europe's collective trauma in the wake of World War II, the right-wing regime having remained officially neutral, but the effect was isolating. With a domestic economy in dire need of investment and a wish to push progressive ideas of 'liberal dictatorship' abroad, Spain's Ministry of Information and Tourism launched its 'Spain is different' ad campaign, promising Europeans temporary respite from the shared pain of recent history through sun, sangria, bullfights and the passion of flamenco. An inspired rebrand, it drew tourists to its sandy coastlines, along with foreign reserves needed to build the new resorts to house them.

This strategy proved more successful than Franco could have hoped, though it led to radical changes to Spain's social customs and visual landscape which would only truly be acknowledged once the country had returned to democracy. Deputy Prime Minister Alfonso Guerra noted that, 'The first tourists to arrive in bikinis did more for the transition than political speeches.' And so despite the fact that, at the time, Benidorm's mayor had been threatened with excommunication for his tolerance of the offending two-pieces, by the 1970s the village had been irreversibly transformed with more than 100 hotels lining its beaches. Mallorca, meanwhile, shifted in less than a generation from an agrarian economy to a predominantly service one. In Clark's shoots for his tour operator clients, he not only captured the Brits' changing mores but the profound shifts occurring in the country which he had chosen to call home. That obliging concierge or attentive camarero you see working at the poolside or behind a bar, despite a white shirt, still has soil beneath his fingernails.

For the most part, Clark photographed real tourists, idling away their time at their hotels; his skill lay in engaging them to help set up his scenography – a girl resting on a lounger here, a man with an air pistol there or a group pose, glasses-in-hand, laughing at a bar. On occasion, he'd use props: a palm leaf dangling in the foreground, say, for a 'tropical' feel where it might be lacking. But whether sat beneath the meringue-like peaks of an Artex ceiling, or half-lost amid the dark leather furniture and patterned carpets of a hotel lounge, all his subjects seem curiously at ease.

Part of this could also be put down to the way they were shot; it wasn't just the flights that got faster and holidays cheaper; photography was subject to the same variables. The industry standard film Kodachrome had given sharpness and accurate colour rendition since the 1930s, but it worked best at slower shutter speeds and required time-consuming and expensive processing. Clark embraced new Ektachrome film with its 'faster' speed for motion shots, which was more suited to flash-free use or interiors. Processing was not only simpler and cheaper, the film sensitivity could be 'pushed' to make it work in lower light conditions – albeit at the expense of higher contrast and lower resolution.

These factors are evident in Clark's work. Freed from the need to be precious with the technology, he amassed thousands of medium-format transparencies of his holidaying subjects engaged in various kinds of leisure activity both inside and out, and at all times of day or night. Unstartled by a flash, they were left to roam freely in a reserve of concrete balconies, full-height glass, orthogonal pools and crazy-paved terrazzo terraces. Fifty years later, here they live, the denizens of a utopian world of municipal civility. Corralled and framed in Ektachrome, Trevor Clark captured British tourists transposed from their dull, grey clime and lures us still into a sun-soaked vision of distorted, grainy technicolour.

Jan-Carlos Kucharek
London, 2024

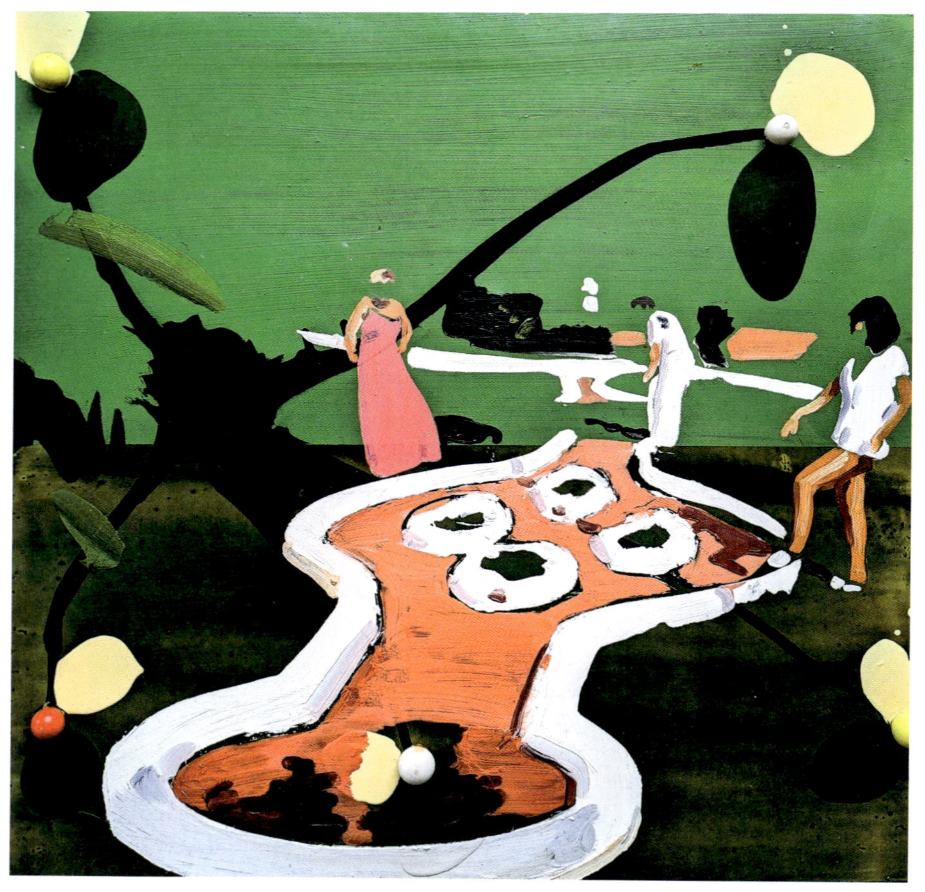

Night Golf, 2001, oil paint and objects on board, 61x61 cm,
by Jake Clark was inspired by one of the photographs
taken by his father, Trevor Clark.

DISCOVERING MY FATHER'S PHOTOGRAPHS

This book is a tribute to my father Trevor Clark, who took every photograph. He worked as a travel and advertising photographer in Mallorca from the 1960s until the 1990s. I lived there as a child and returned to England in 1975, when my parents separated. Most of my summer holidays were spent staying with Trevor at his house in Portals Nous, near one of the main resorts. From the roof you could see the flickering lights of Palma Nova and Magaluf, where I did a lot of partying as a teenager.

I would help him on photo shoots sometimes, which led me to study photography before eventually deciding to pursue painting for my BA and MA courses. Around this time, in the early 1990s, I discovered Trevor's archive and started to spend hours looking through the thousands of transparencies he shot for travel brochures. It was a treasure trove of intriguing imagery, and before too long I began painting from them. I was drawn to the lurid colours and tanned tourists lounging in front of hotels or pursuing leisure activities. I used collaged linoleum and domestic materials as a way of breaking up the surface, which, along with the painting process itself, gave an emotional charge to the idealised images of holiday heaven. The painting here uses plastic balls to subvert the tranquil game of mini golf.

I am not sure whether my father totally understood my fascination with his photographs of package holidays. For me, they act as a link to my childhood in Mallorca – my brother and I are in some of them, posing around a pool or on a beach. Trevor died in 2018 and these images mean a lot to me. They are a way of connecting with him, both as his son and as an artist. This is the first time that this extensive archive of images has been published.

Jake Clark
London, 2024

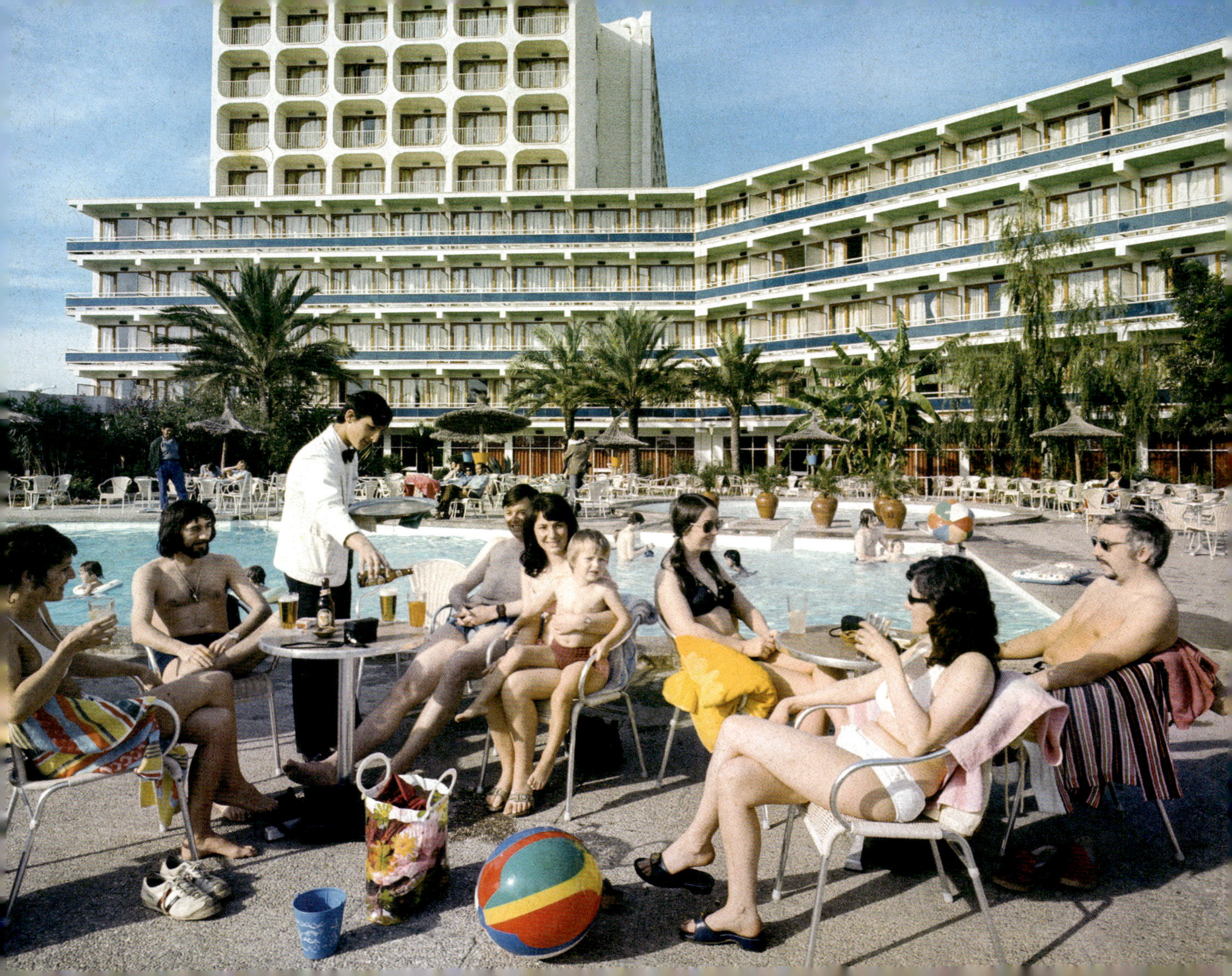

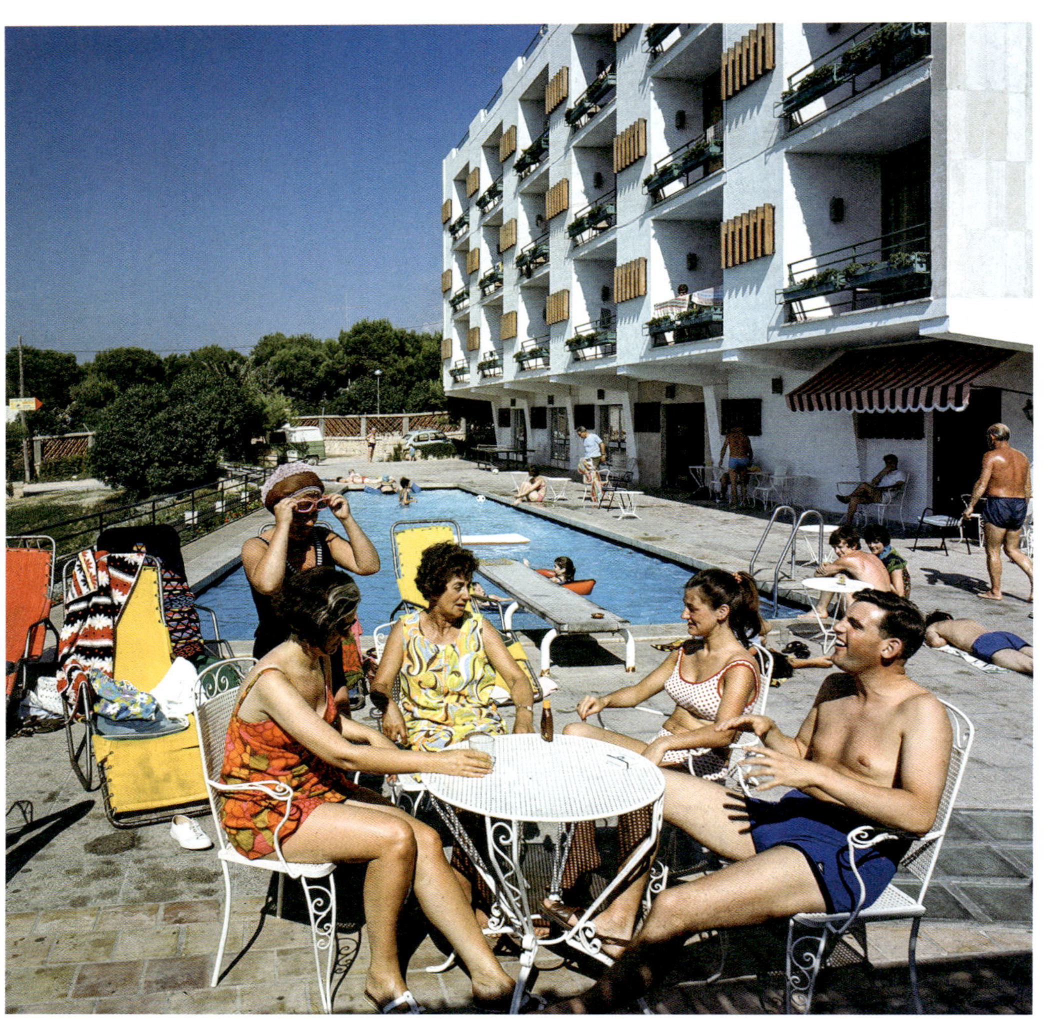

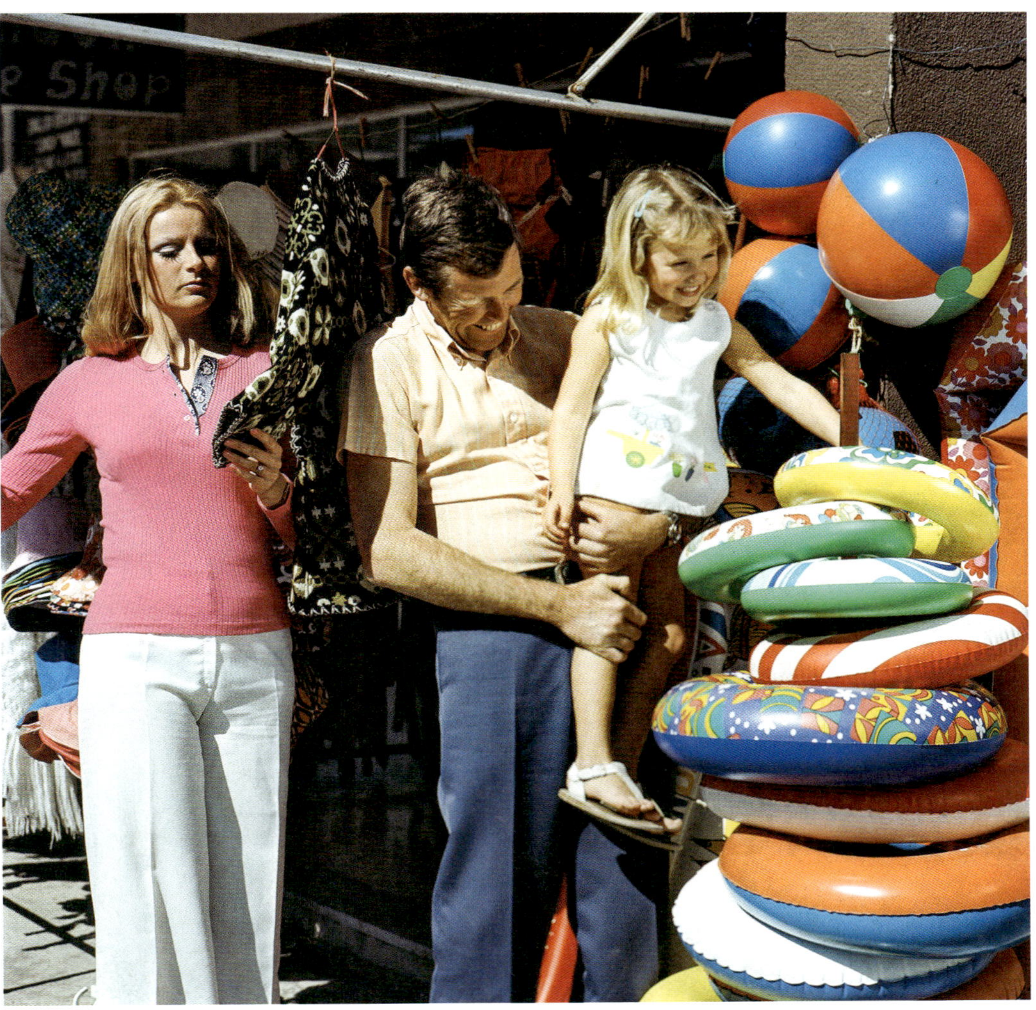
e Shop

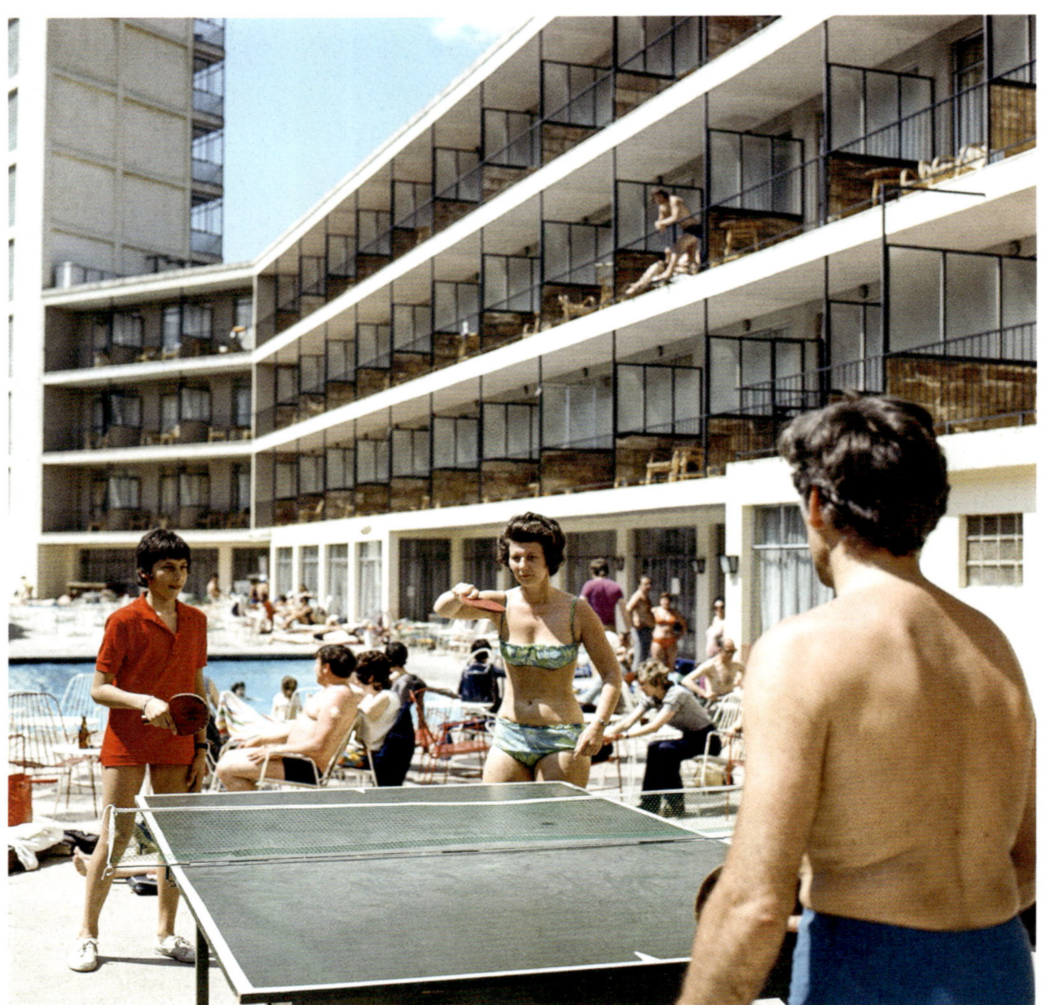

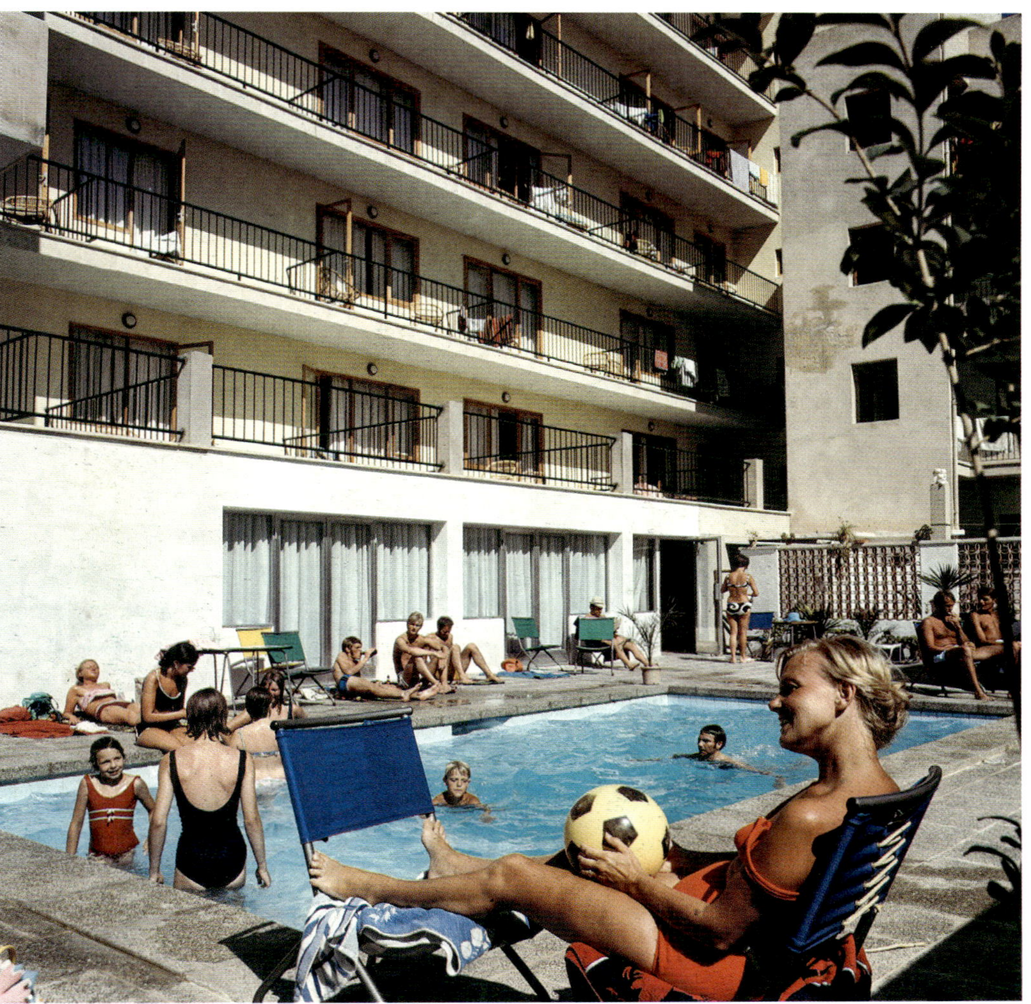

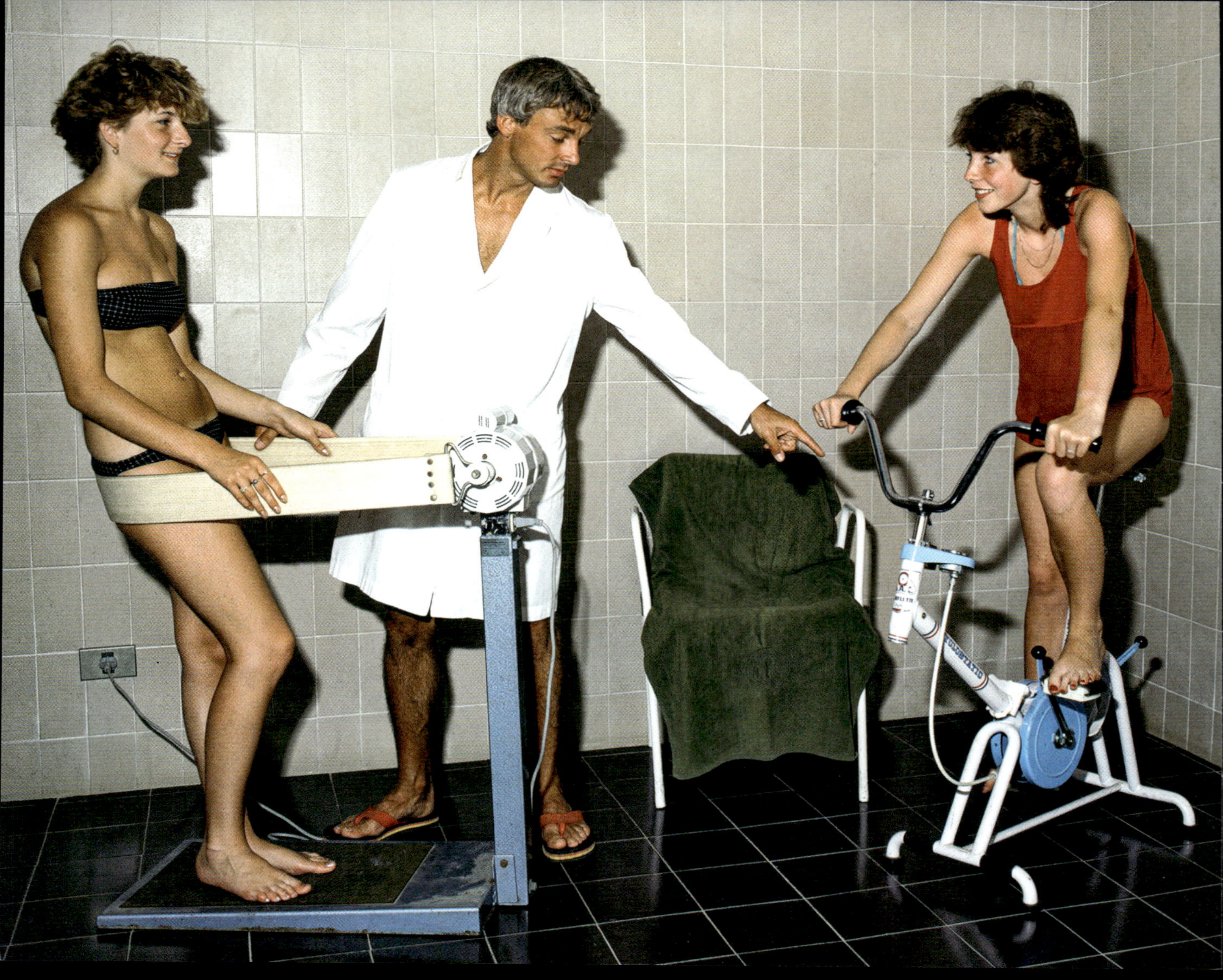

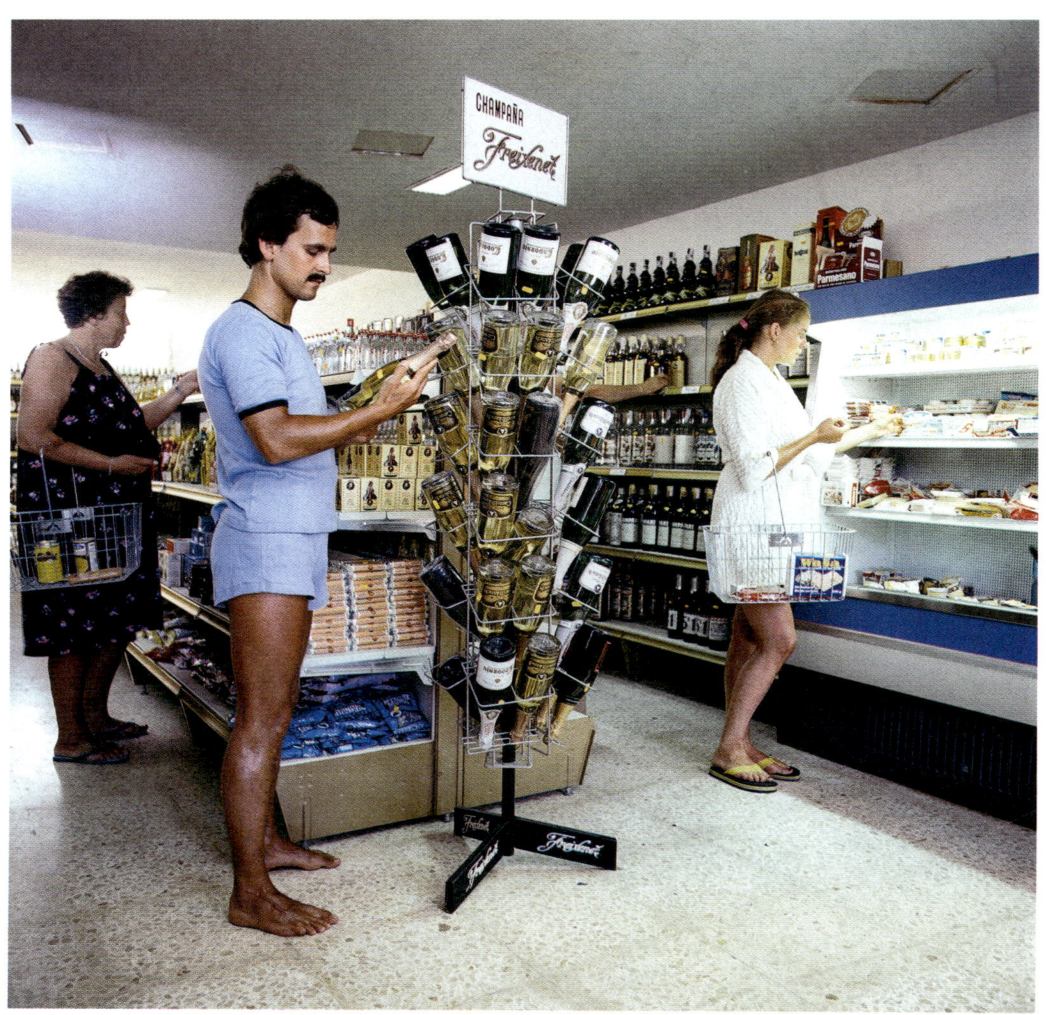
CHAMPAÑA
Freixenet
Freixenet
Freixenet
Parmesano

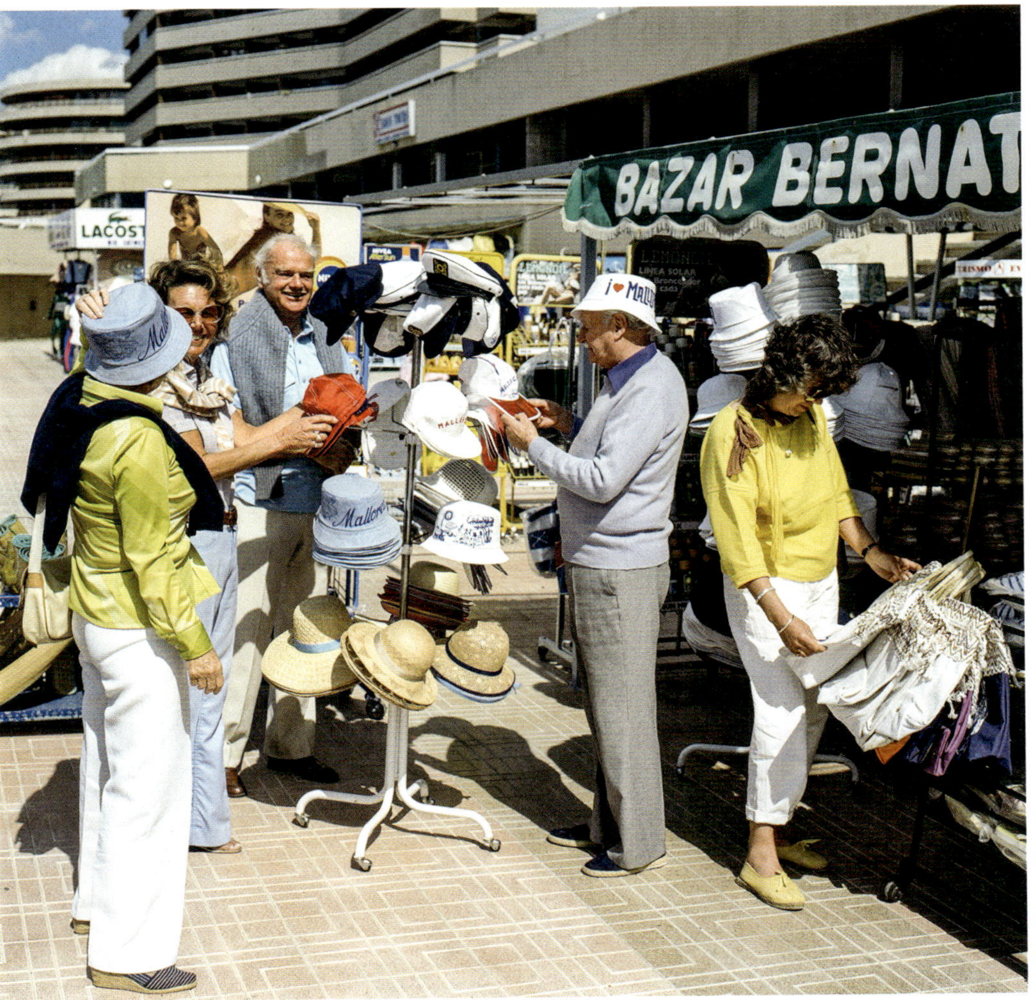

LACOSTE
BAZAR BERNAT
I ♥ MALLORCA
Mallorca
Mallorca

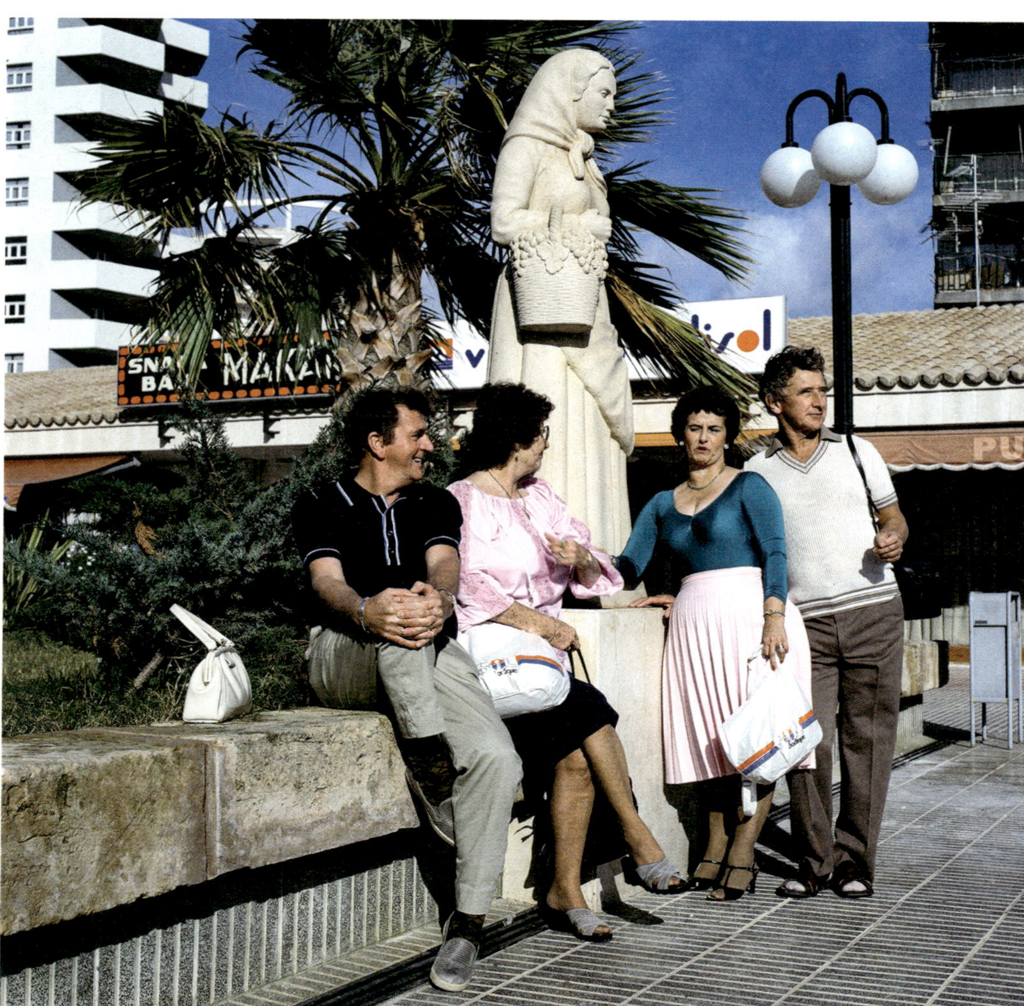

SNACK MAKAN
BAR MAKAN
isol

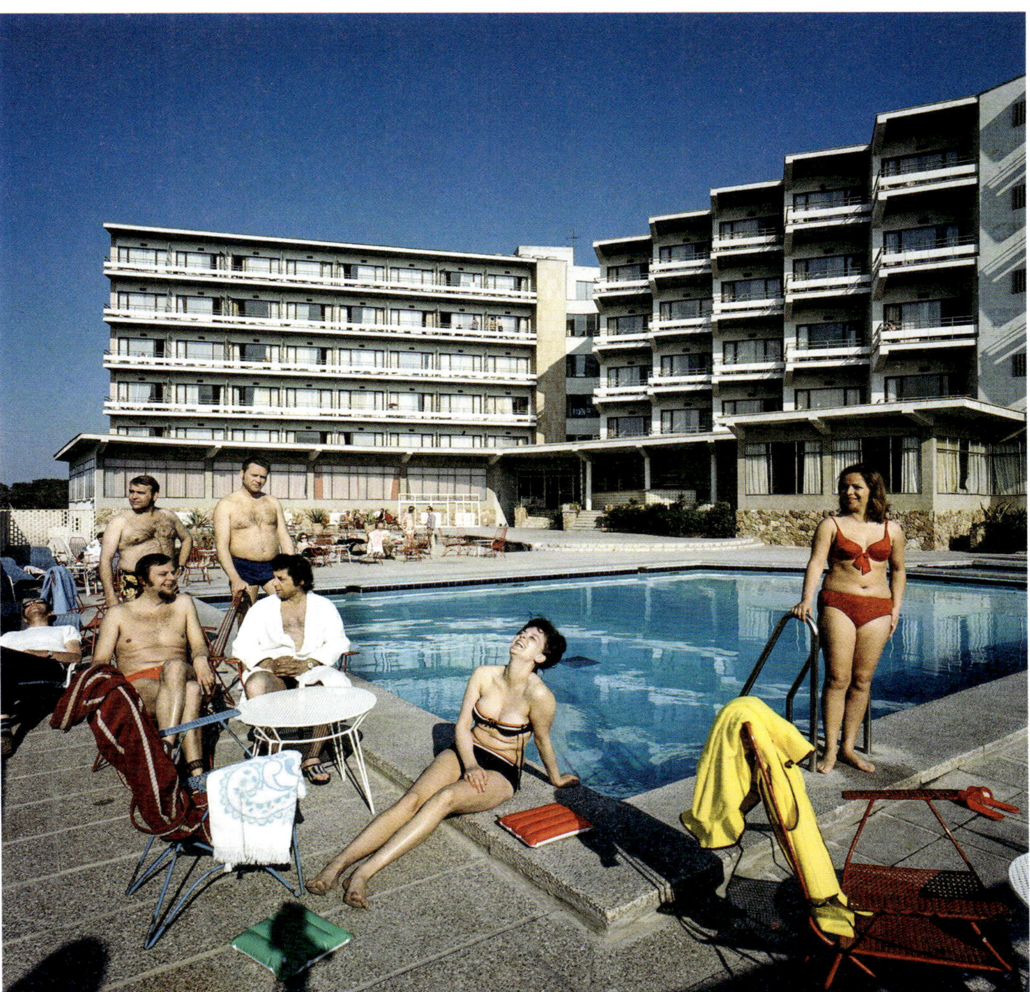

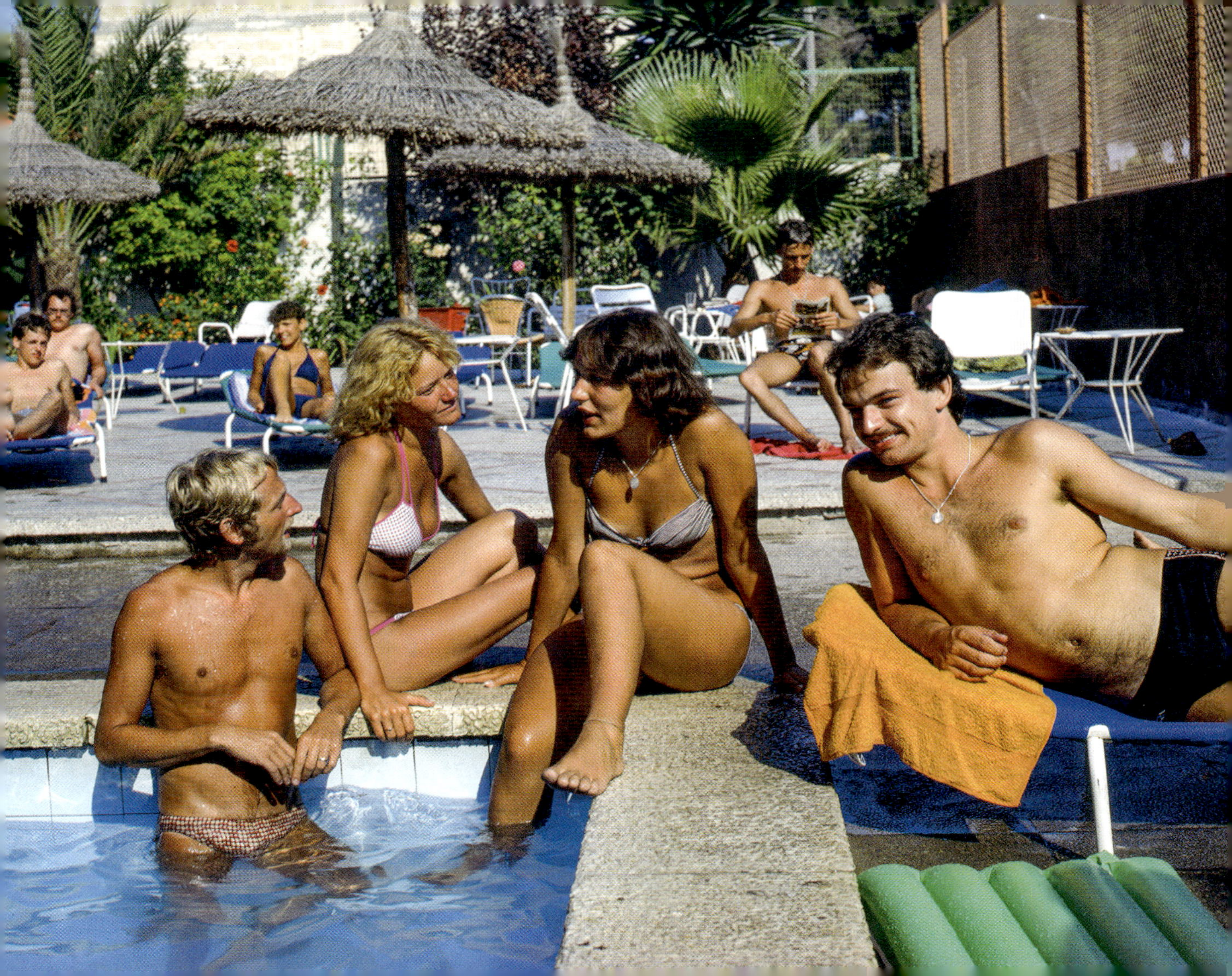

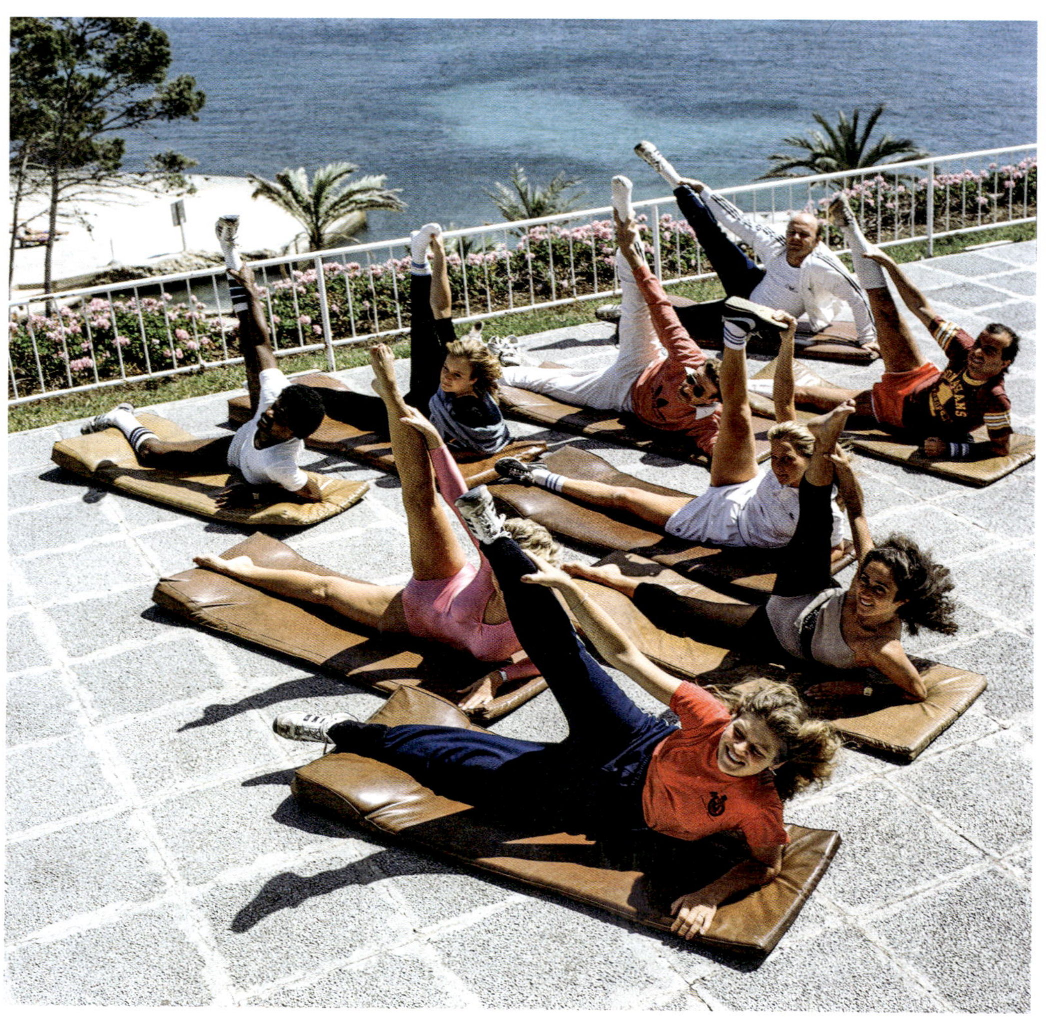

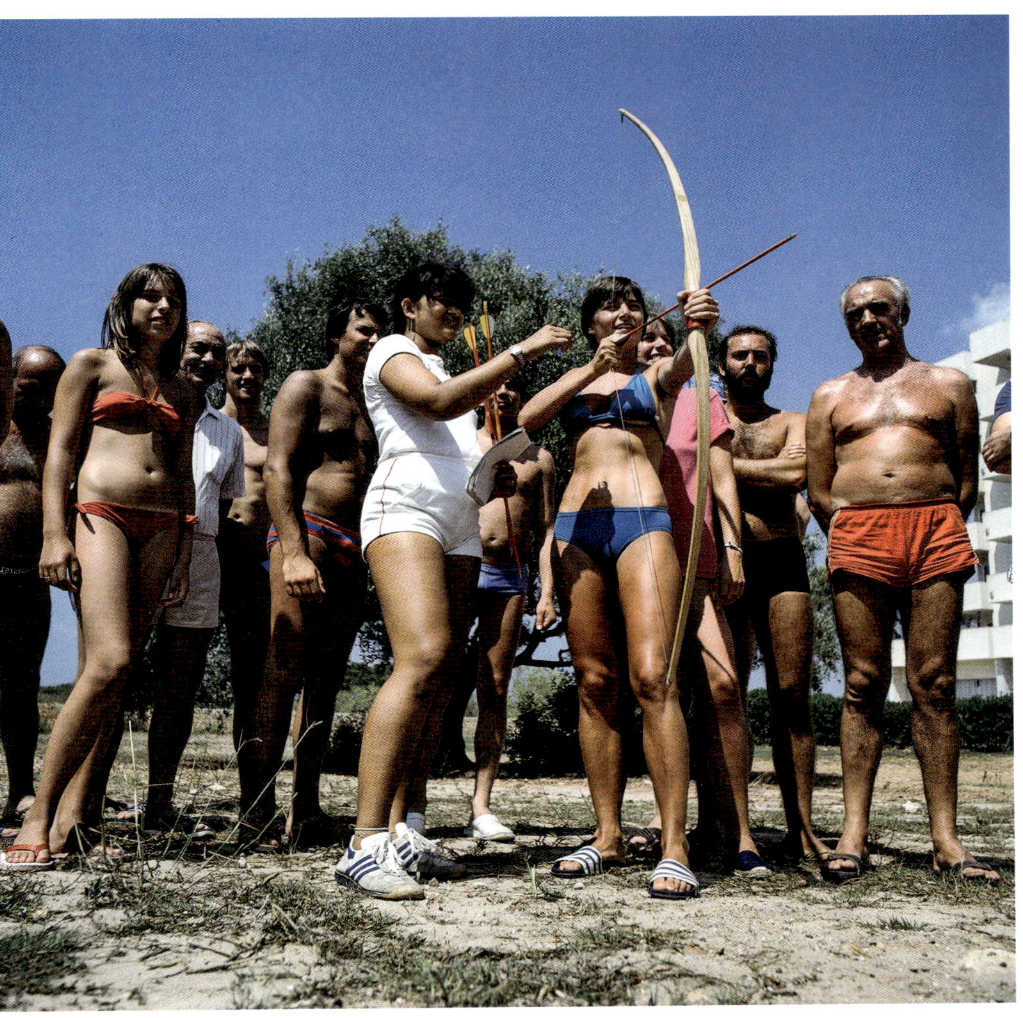

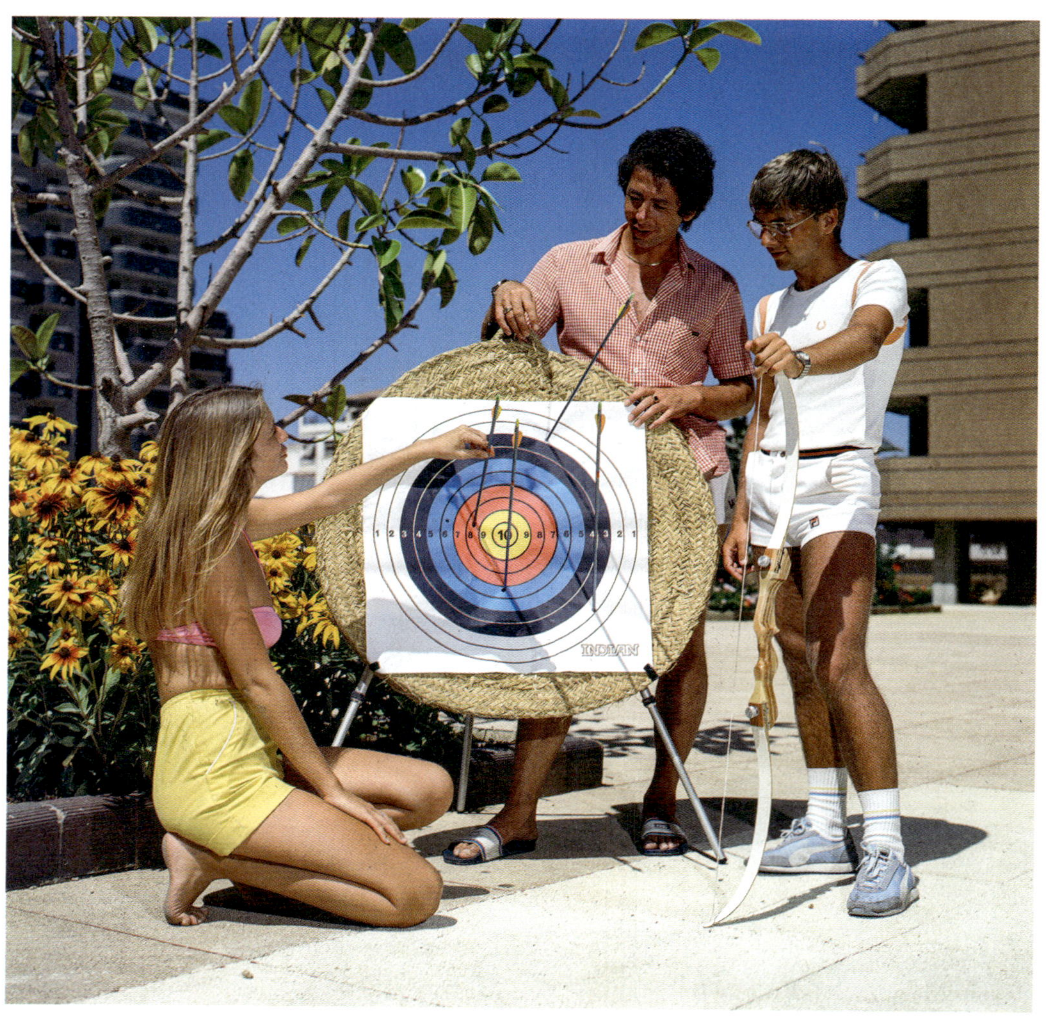

1 2 3 4 5 6 7 8 9 10 9 8 7 6 5 4 3 2 1
INDIAN

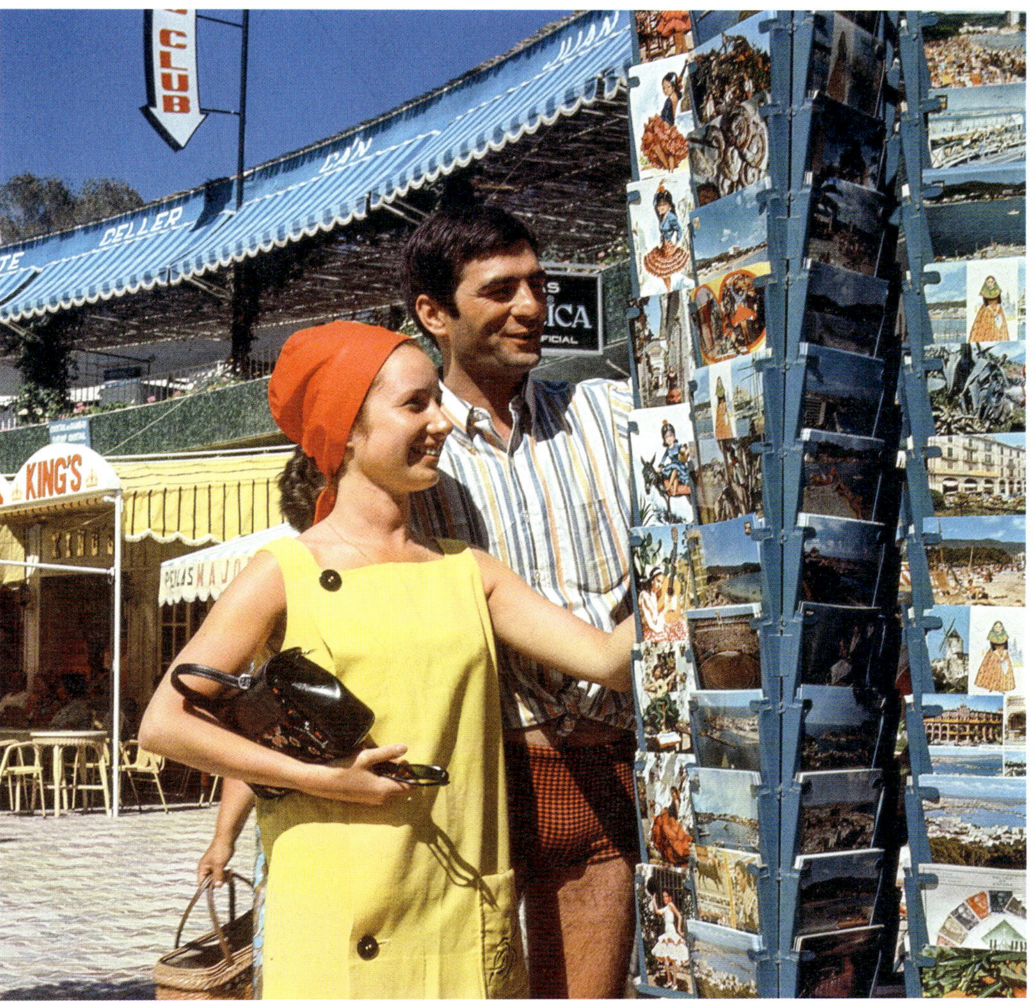

CLUB
DELLER
KING'S

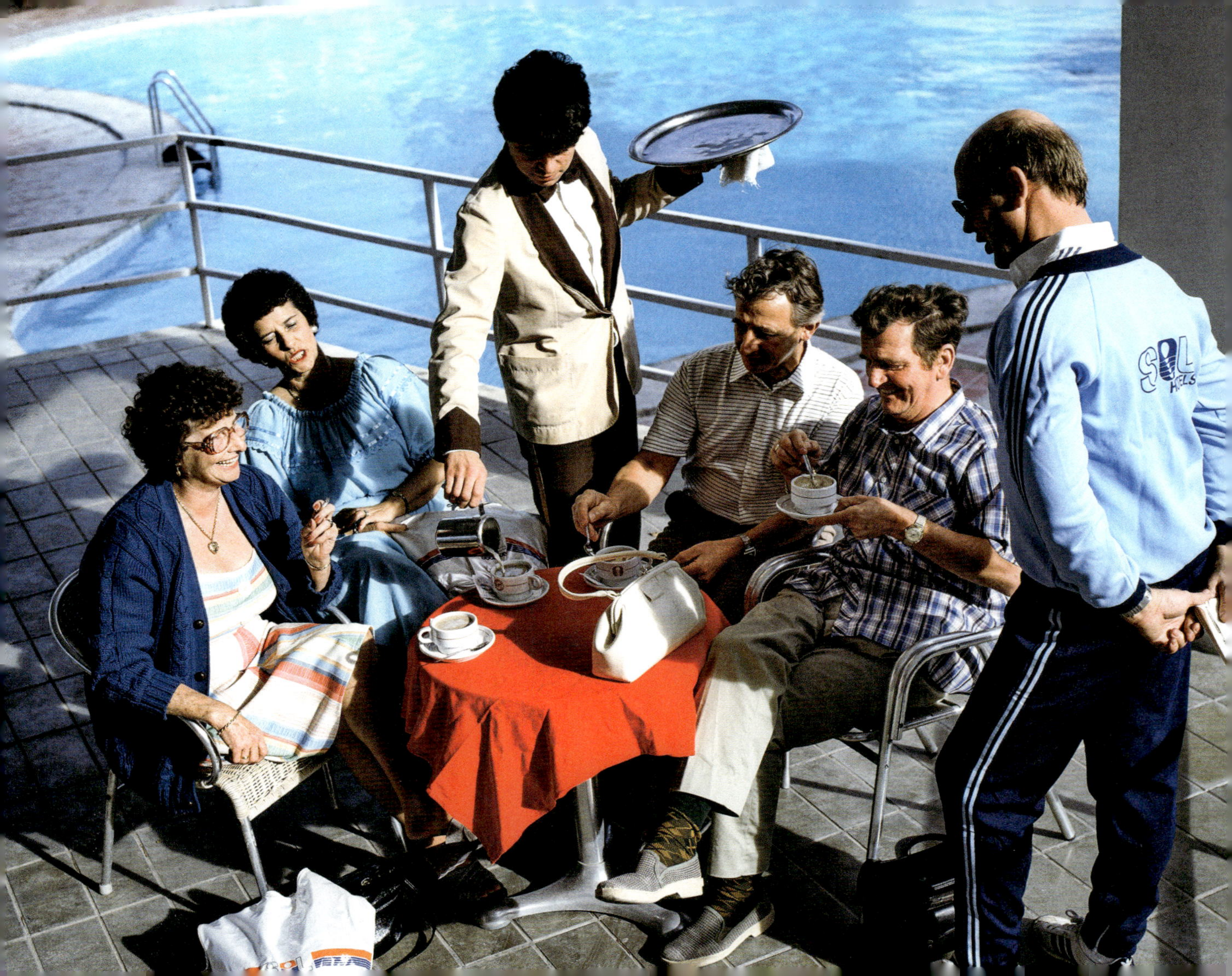
SOL
HOTELS

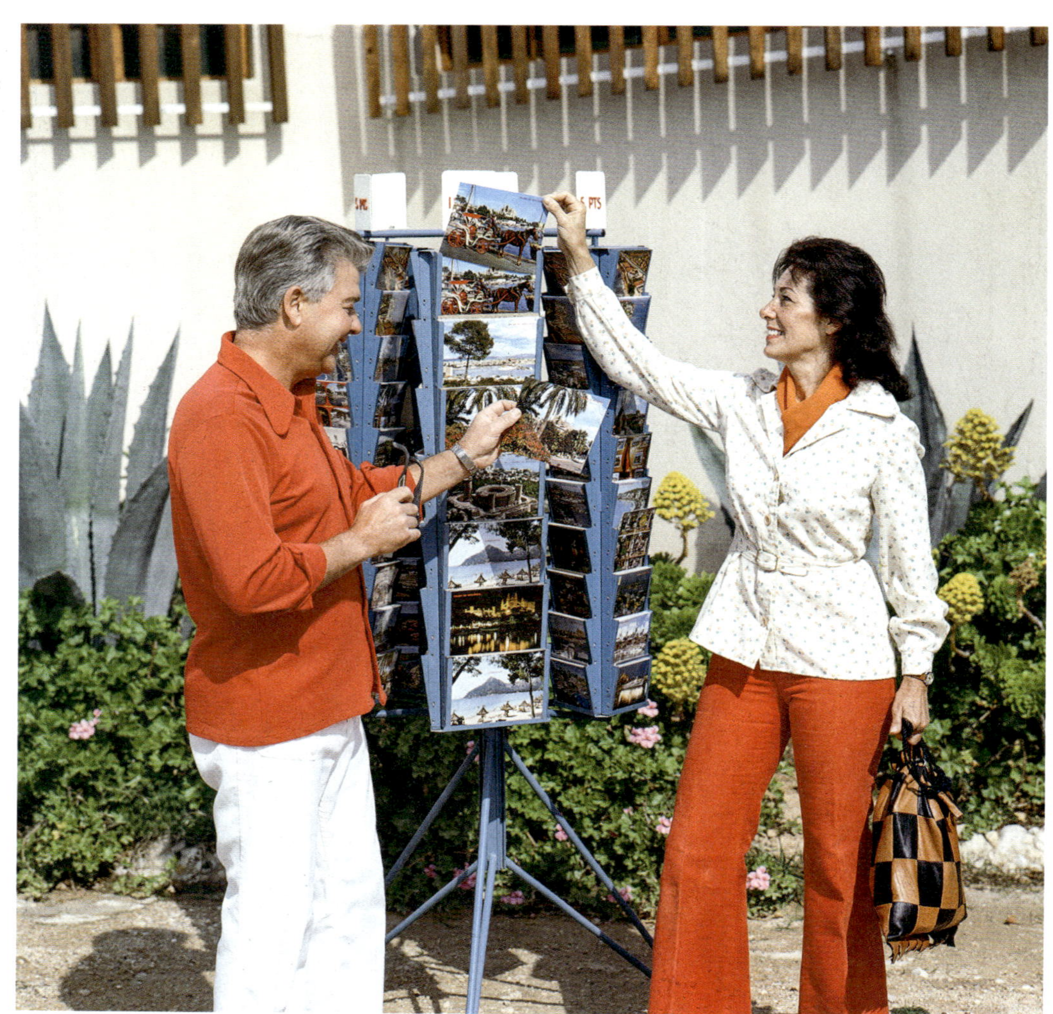
PTS

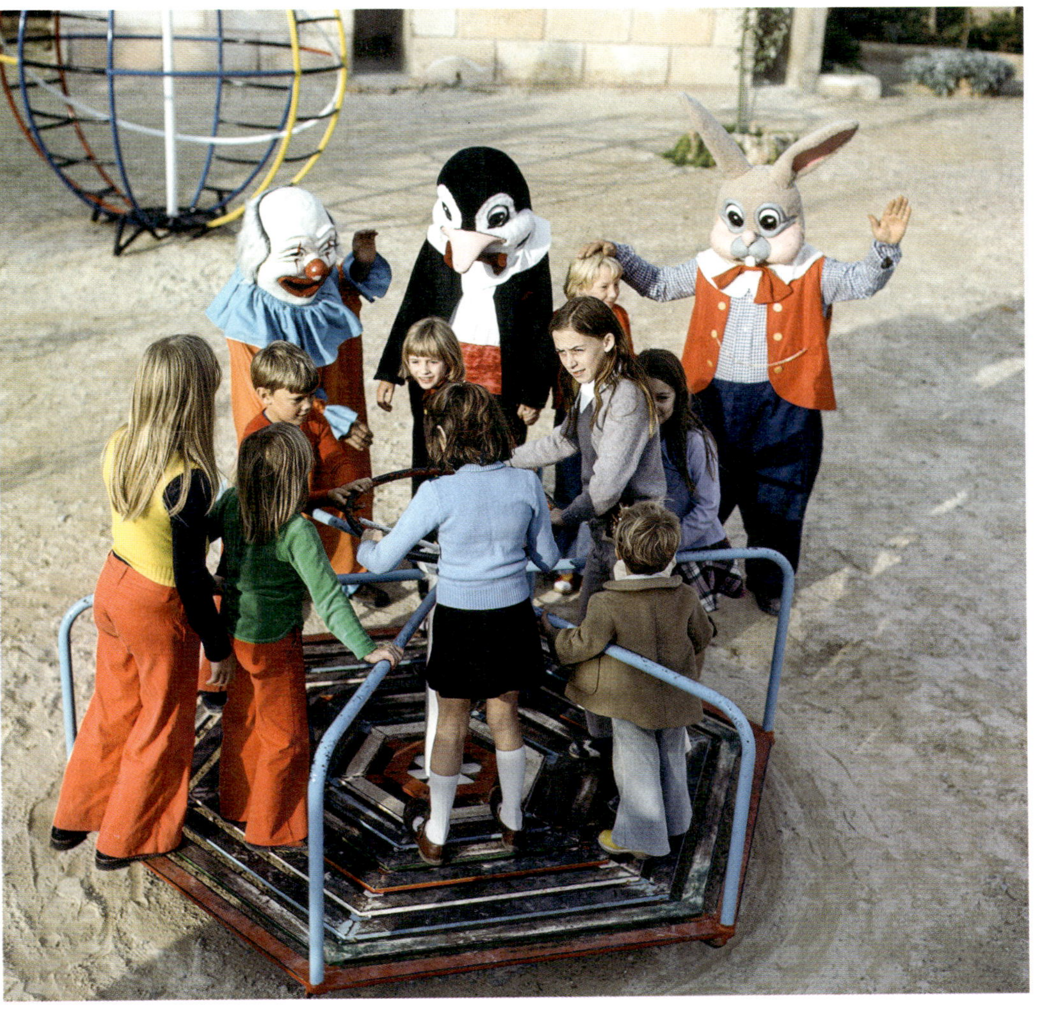

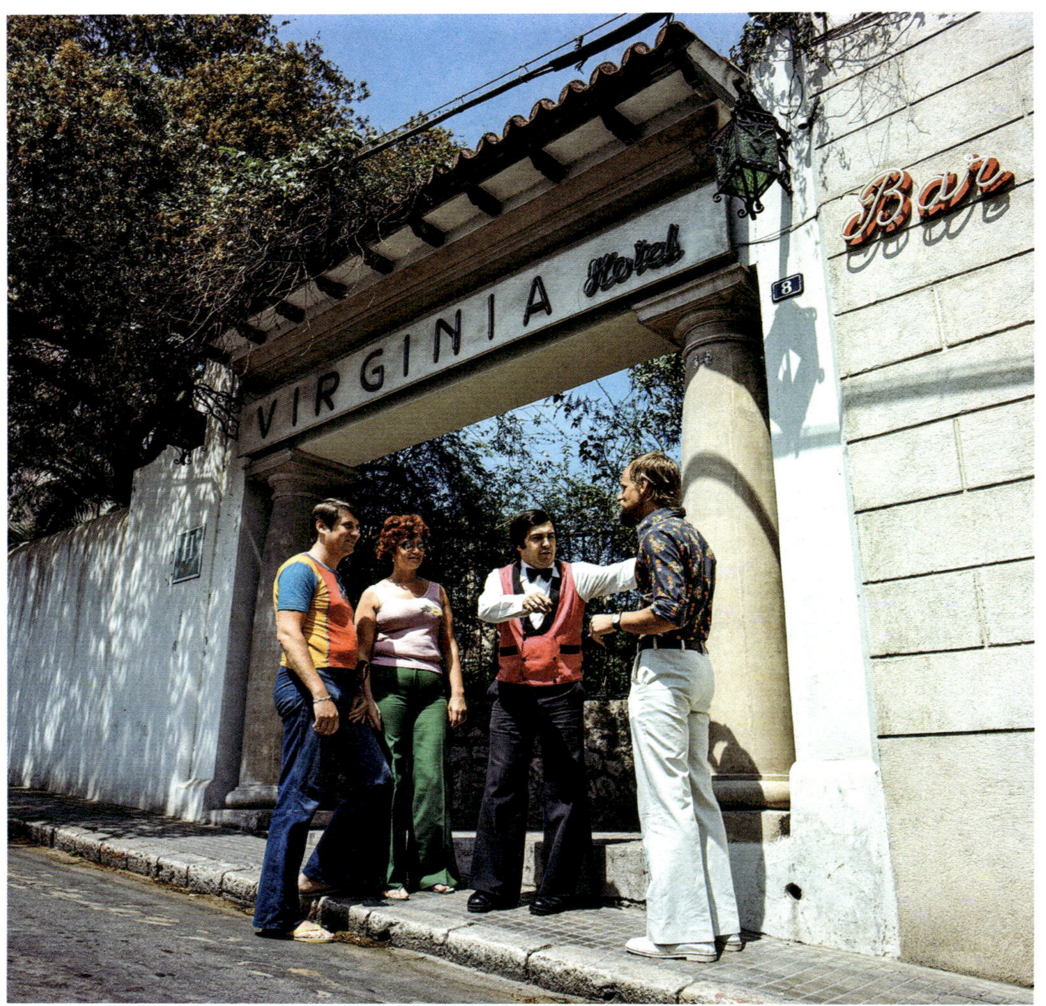

VIRGINIA Hotel
Bar
8

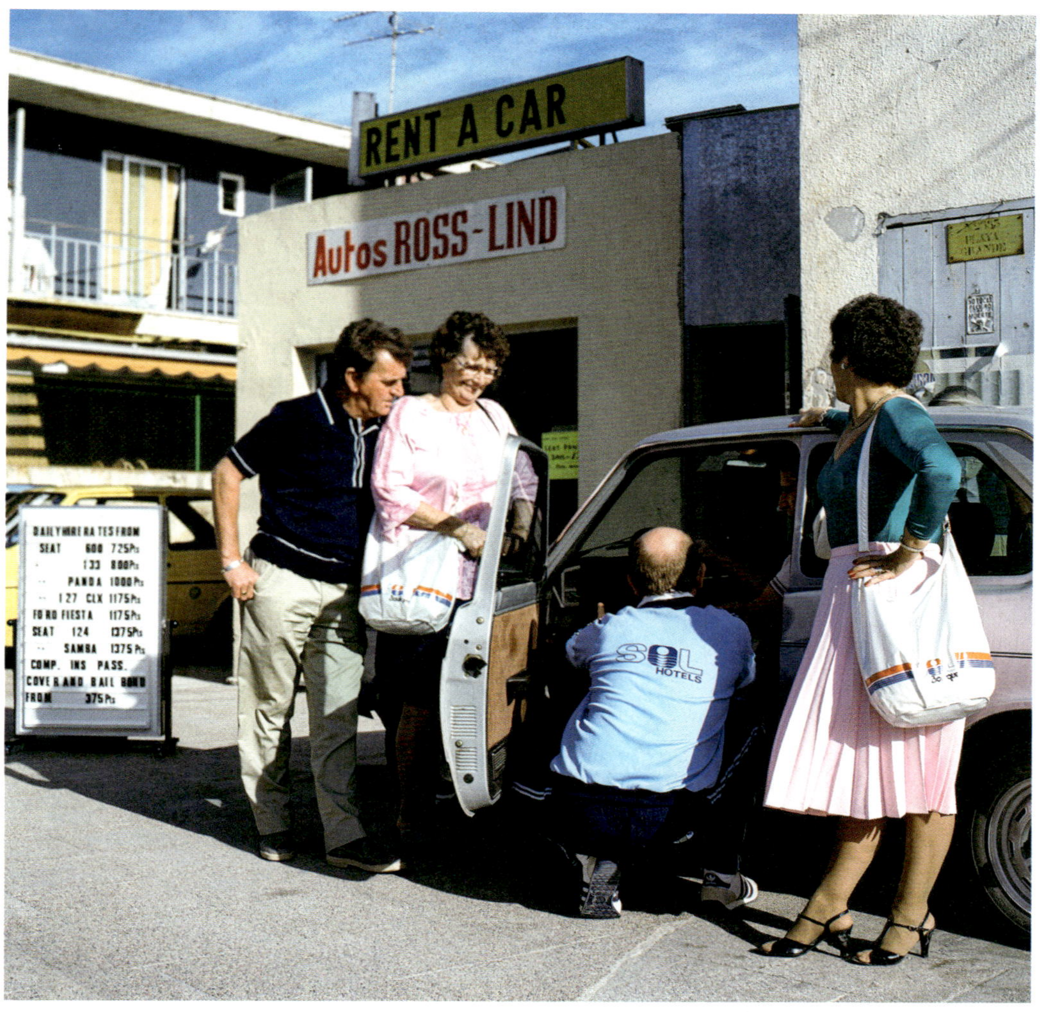

RENT A CAR
Autos ROSS-LIND
DAILY HIRE RATES FROM
SEAT   600   725Pts
..   133   800Pts
..   PANDA   1000Pts
..   127 CLX   1175Pts
FORD FIESTA   1175Pts
SEAT   124   1375Pts
..   SAMBA   1375Pts
COMP. INS PASS.
COVER AND BAIL BOND
FROM   375Pts
SOL HOTELS

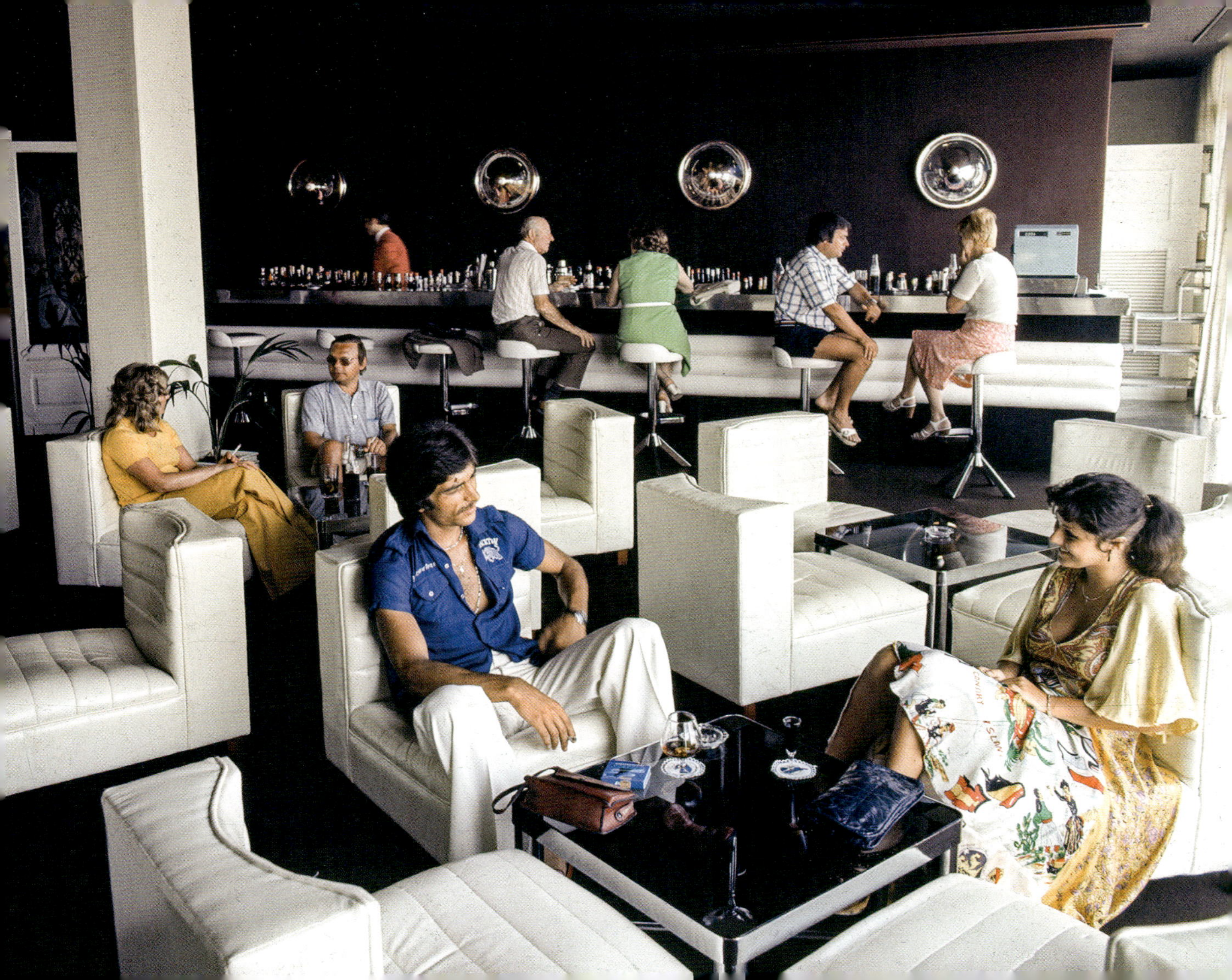

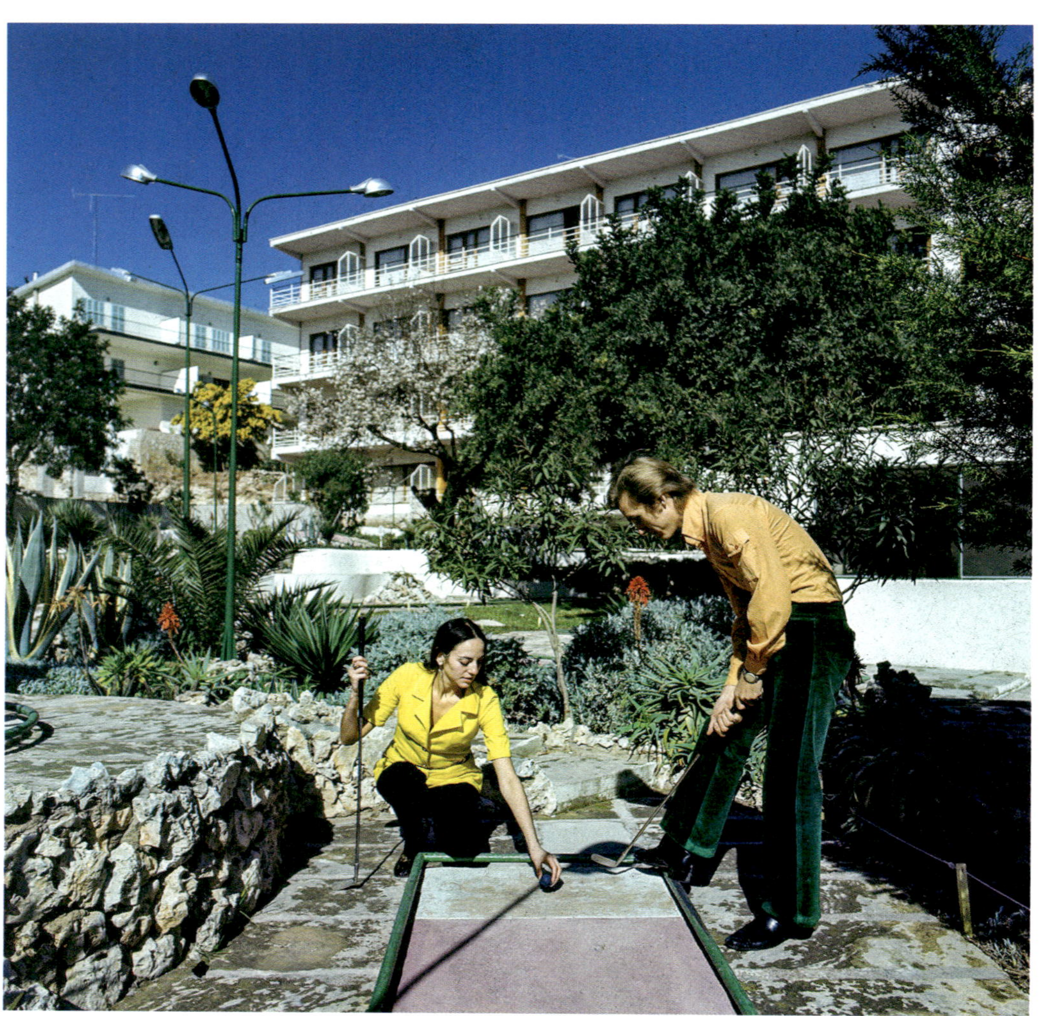

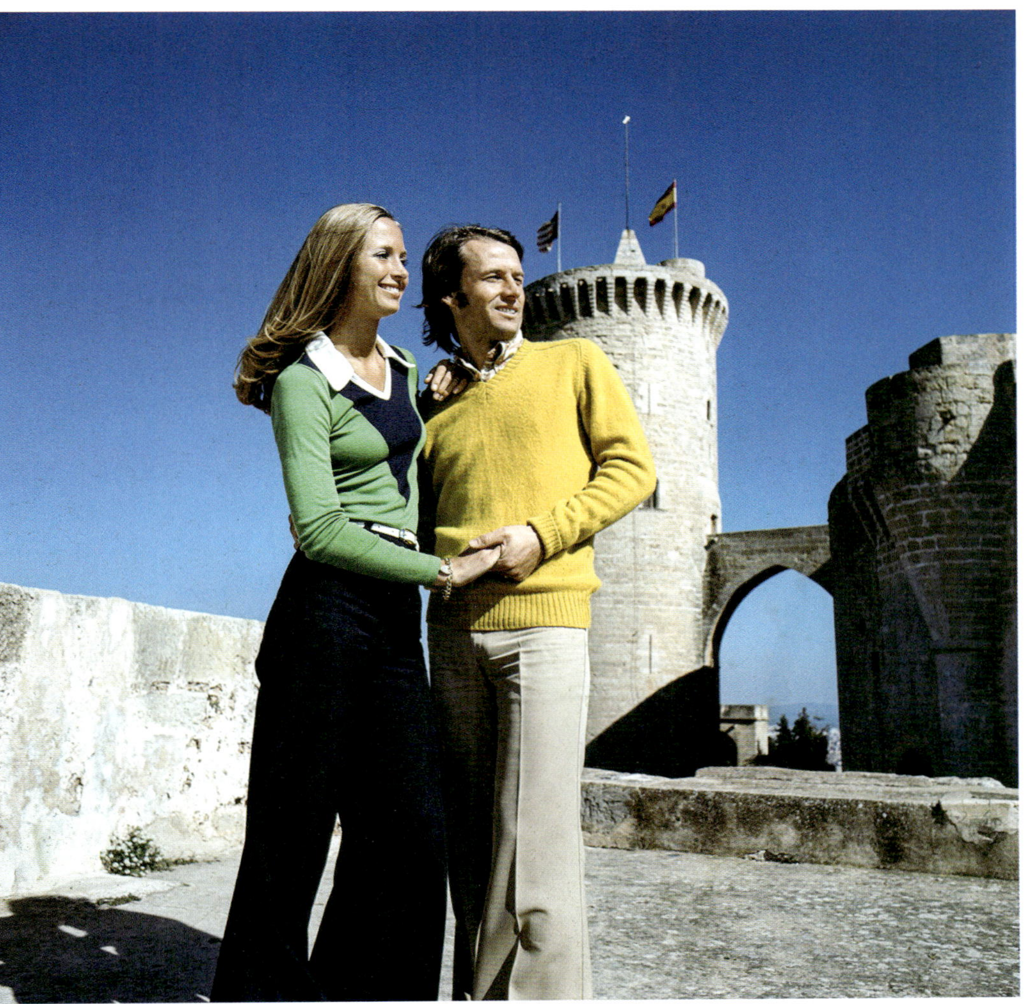

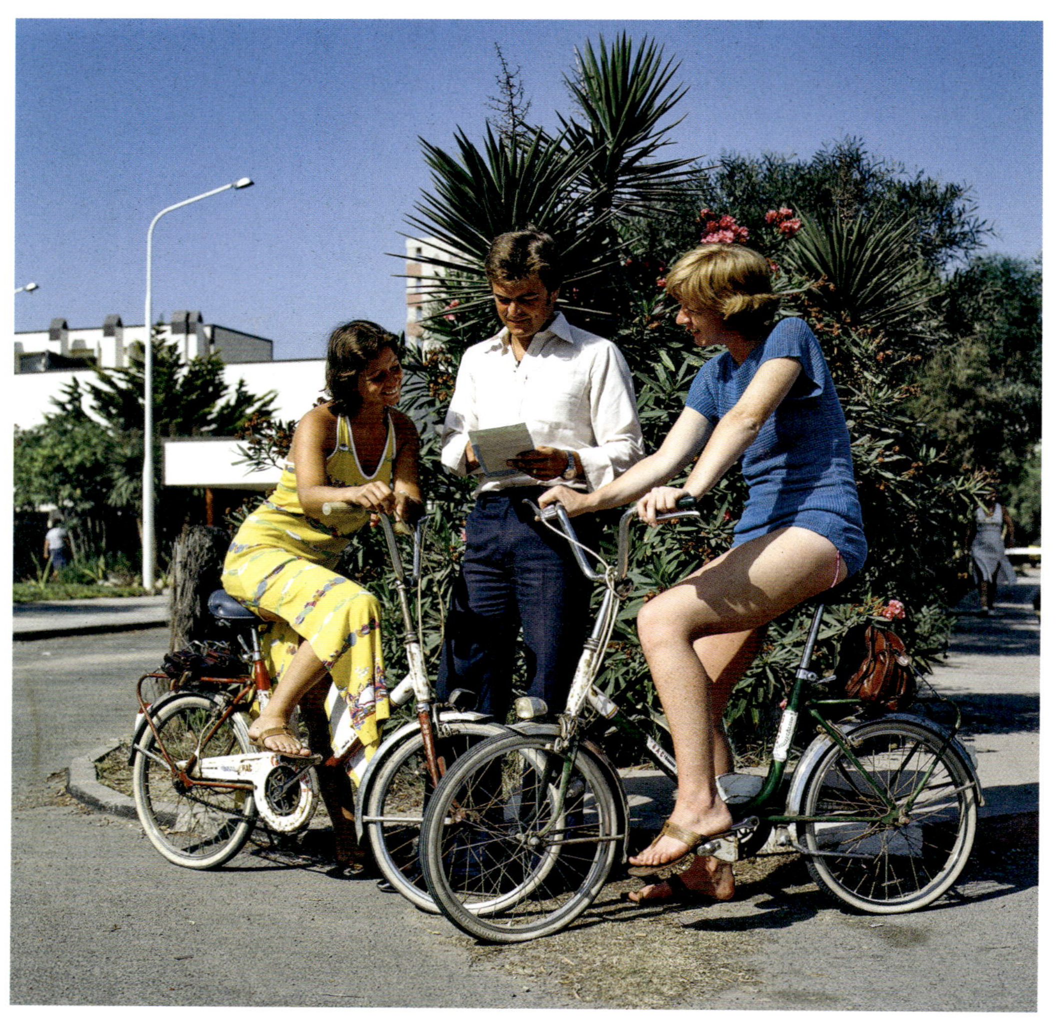

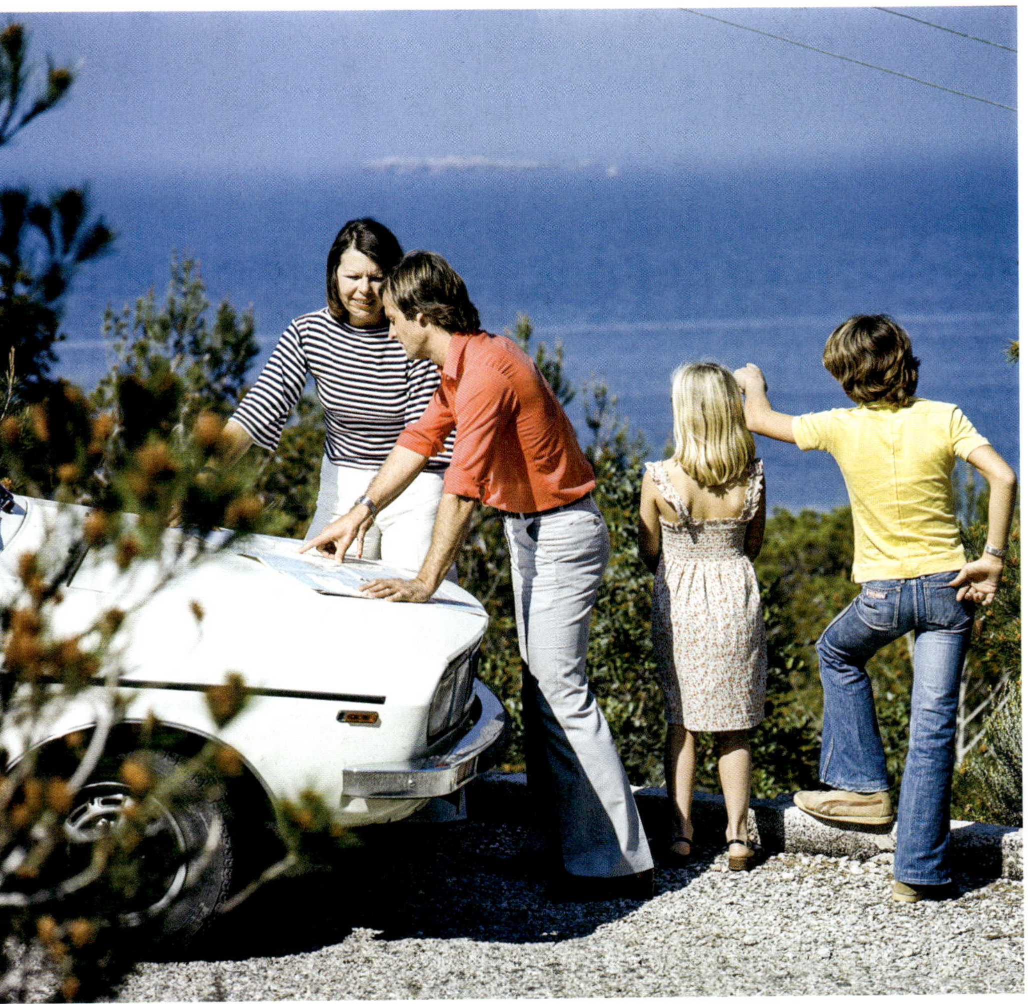

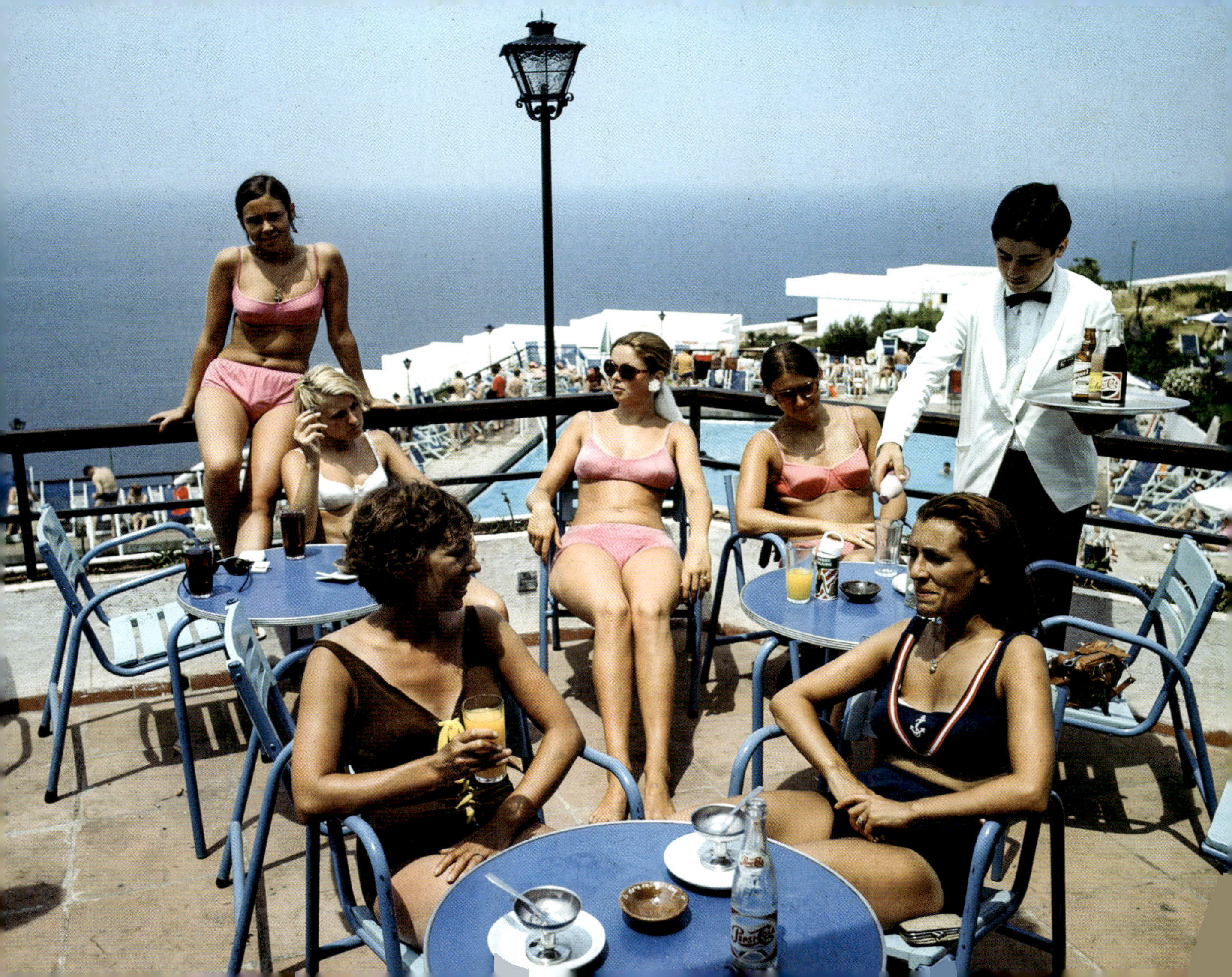

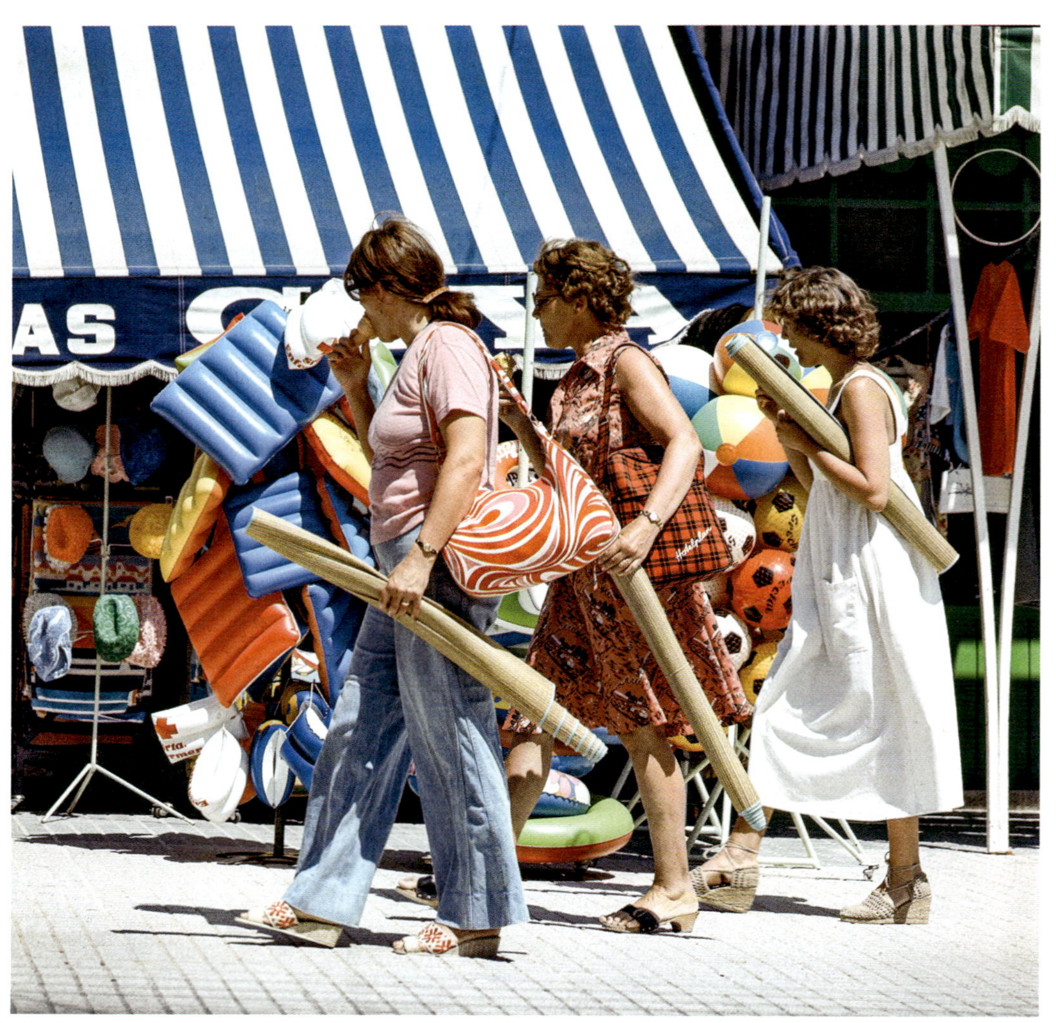
AS
S

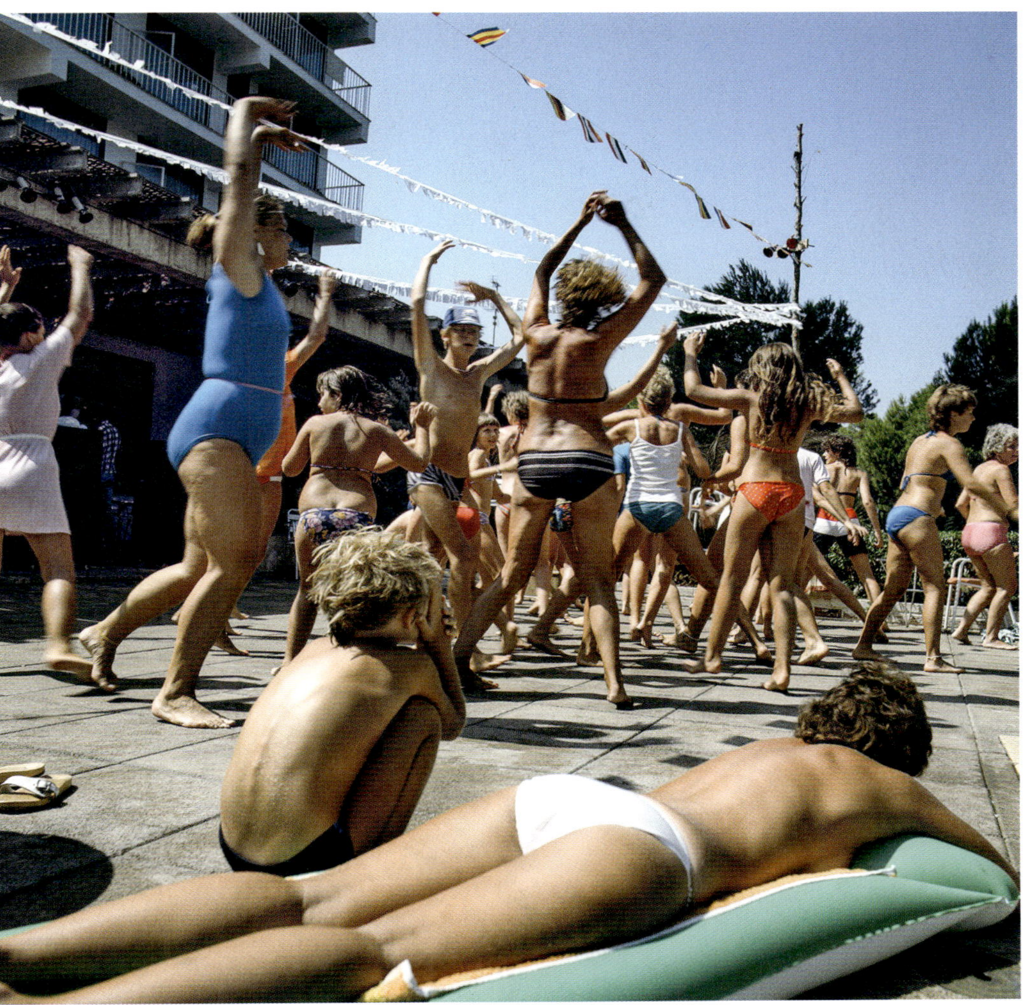

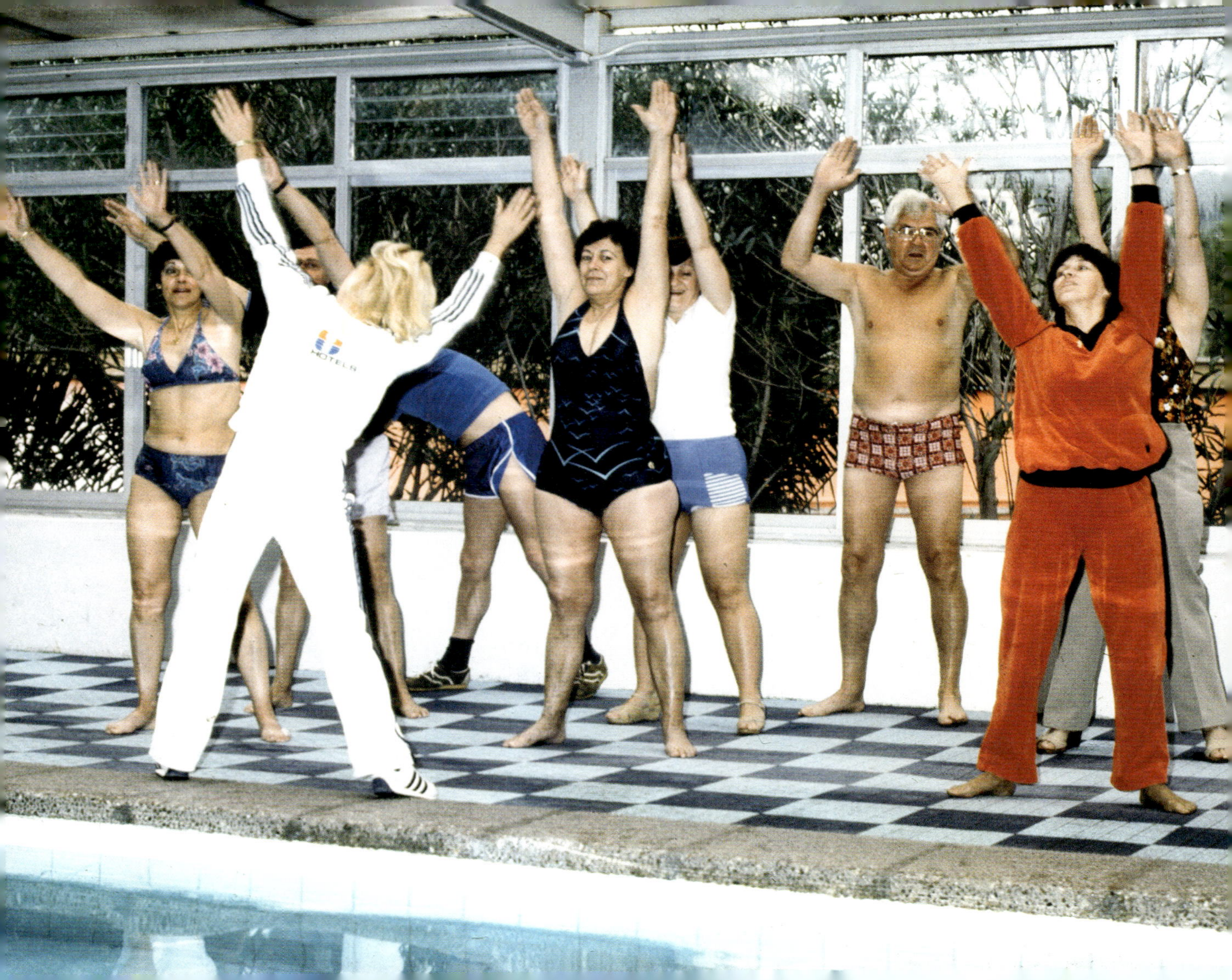

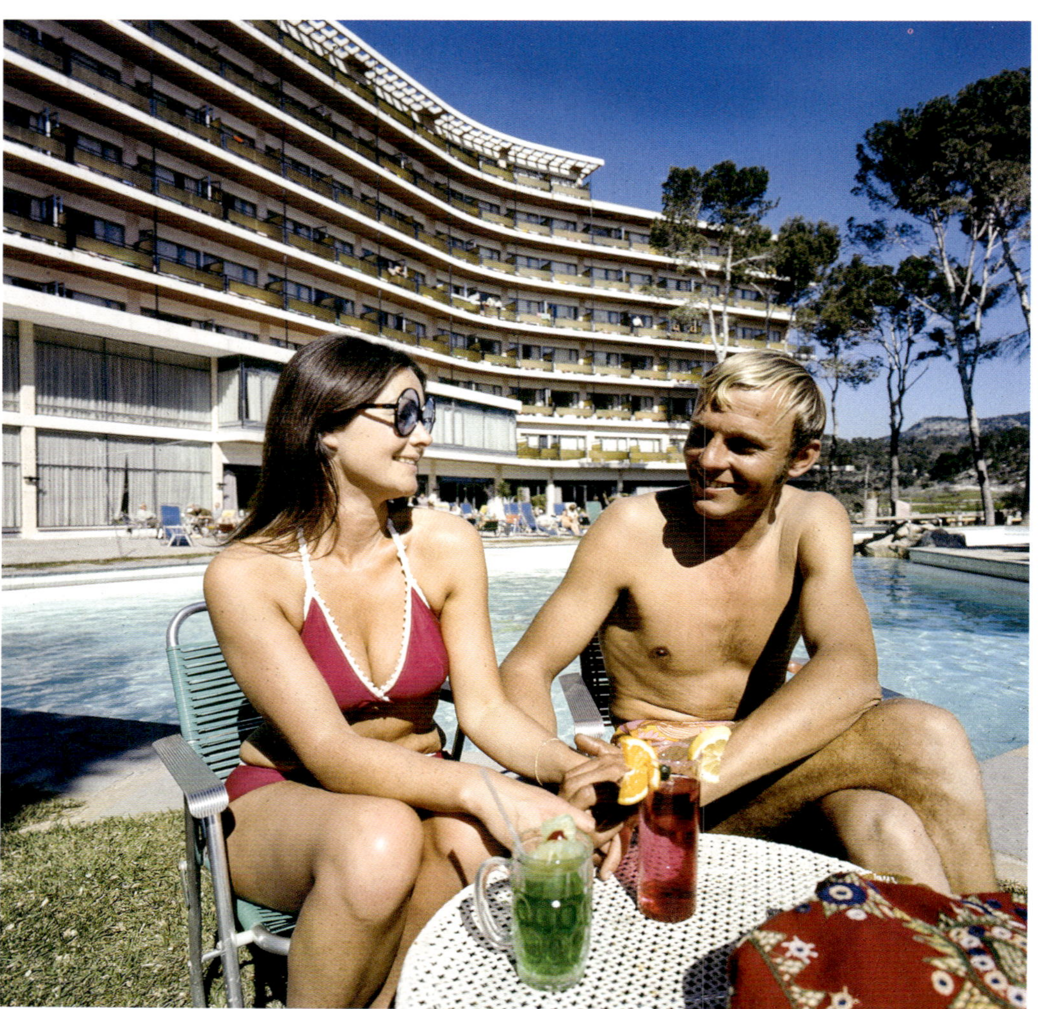

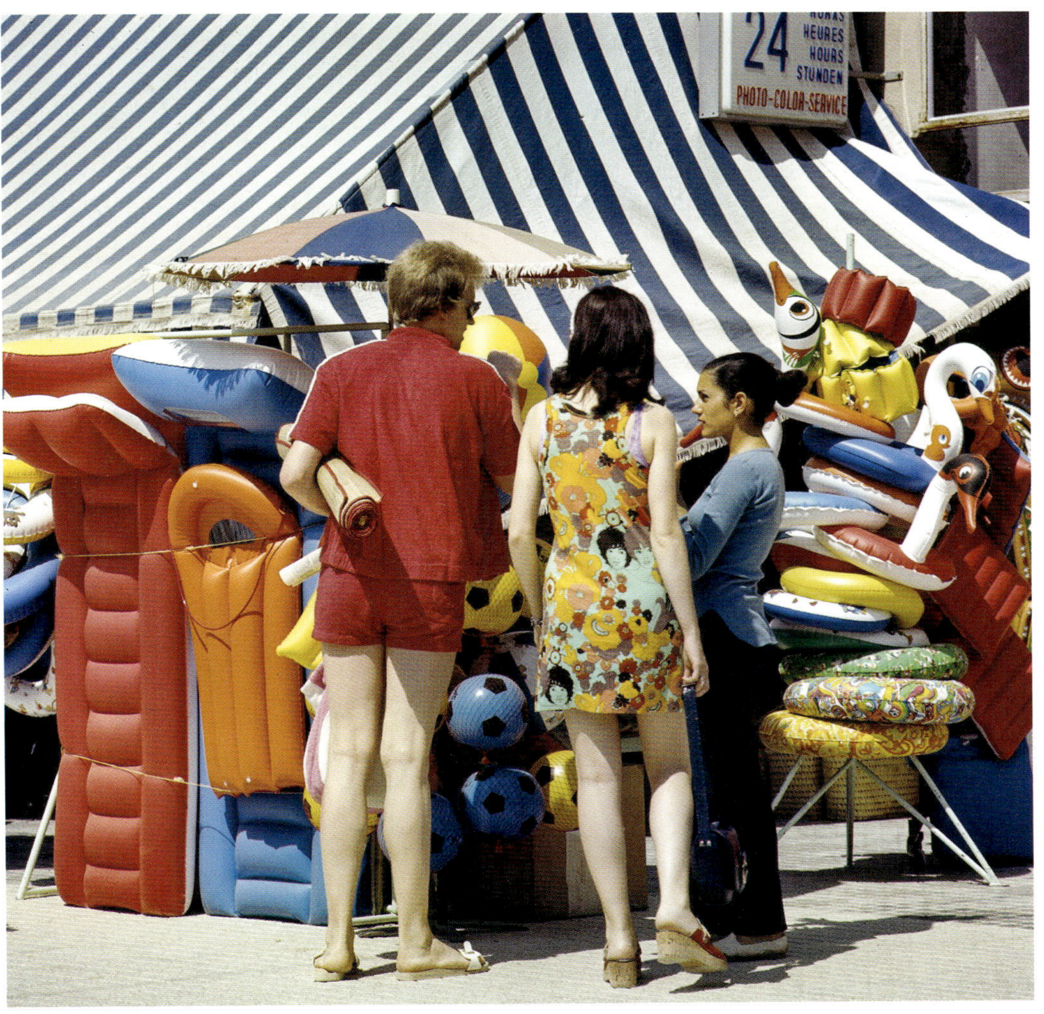
24
HORAS
HEURES
HOURS
STUNDEN
PHOTO-COLOR-SERVICE

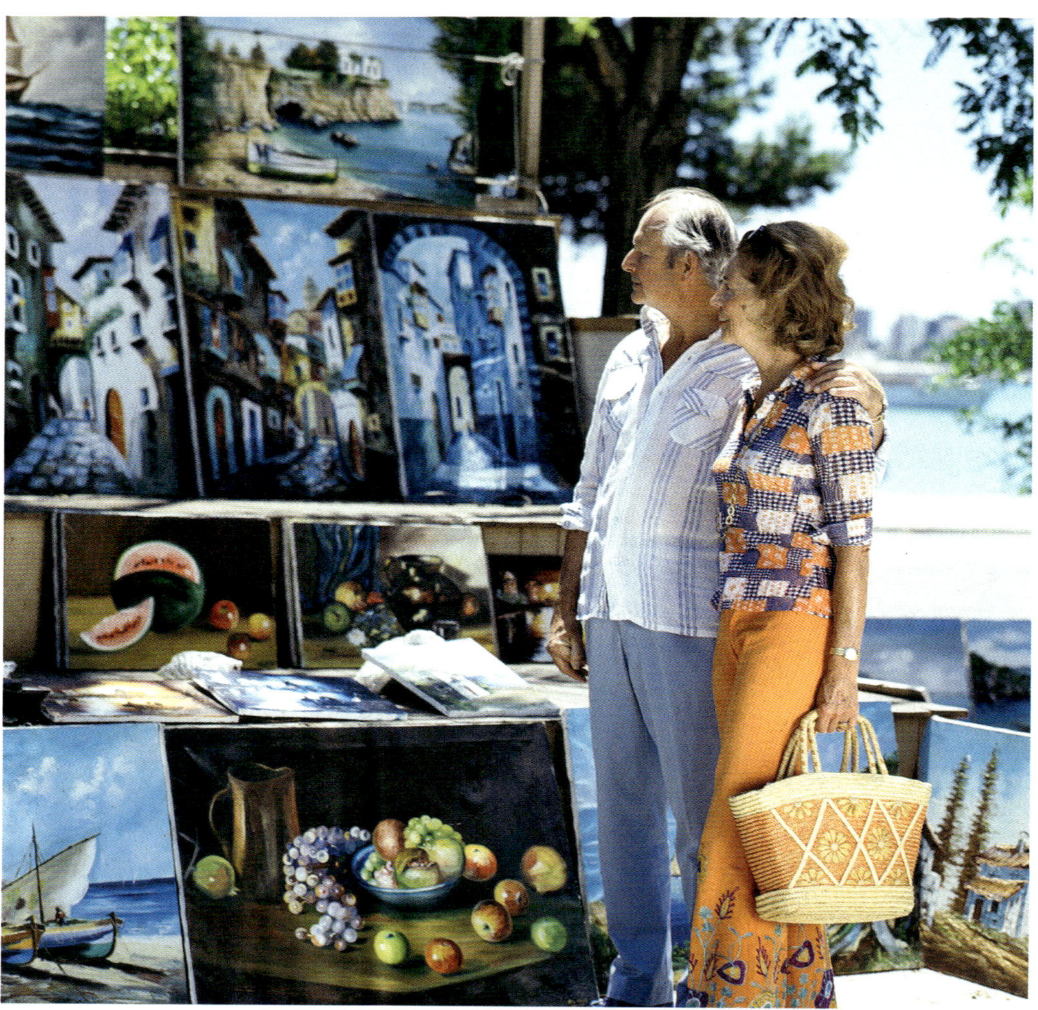

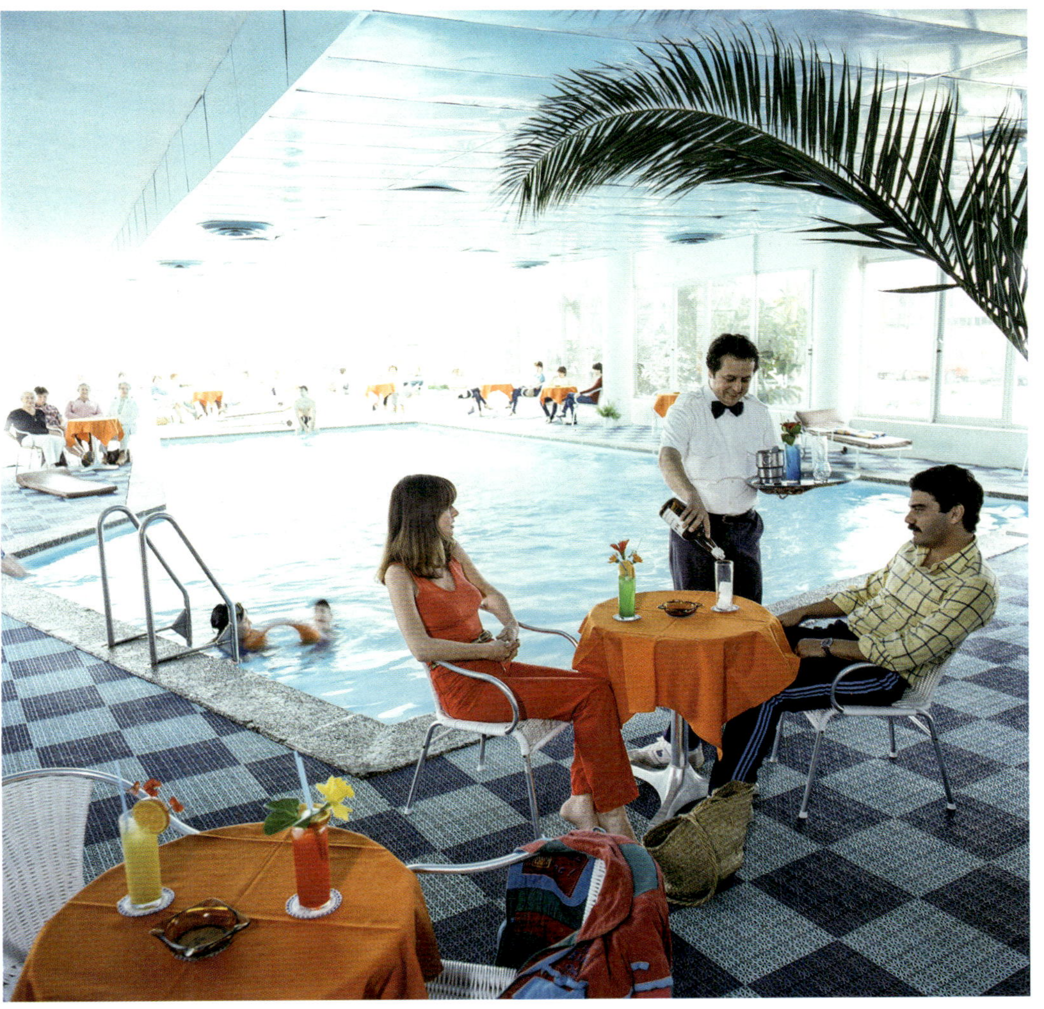

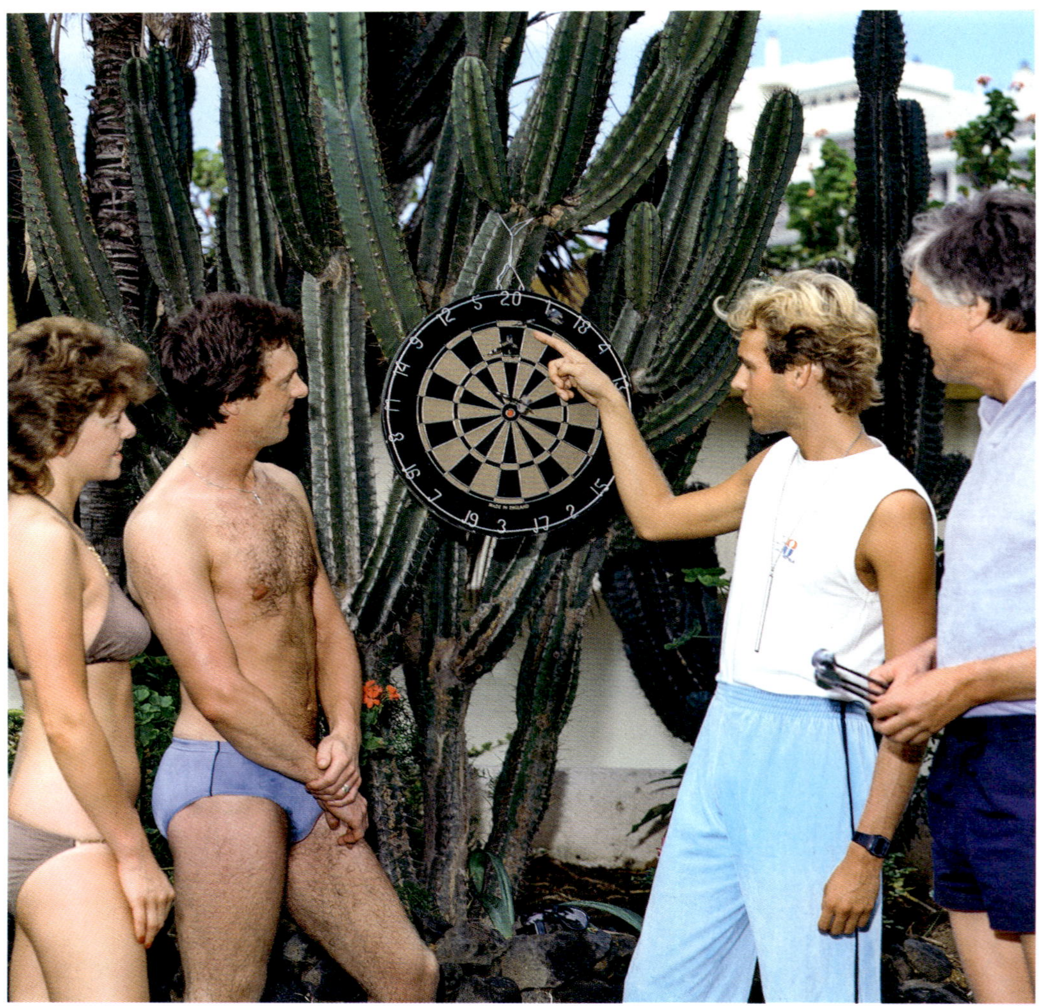

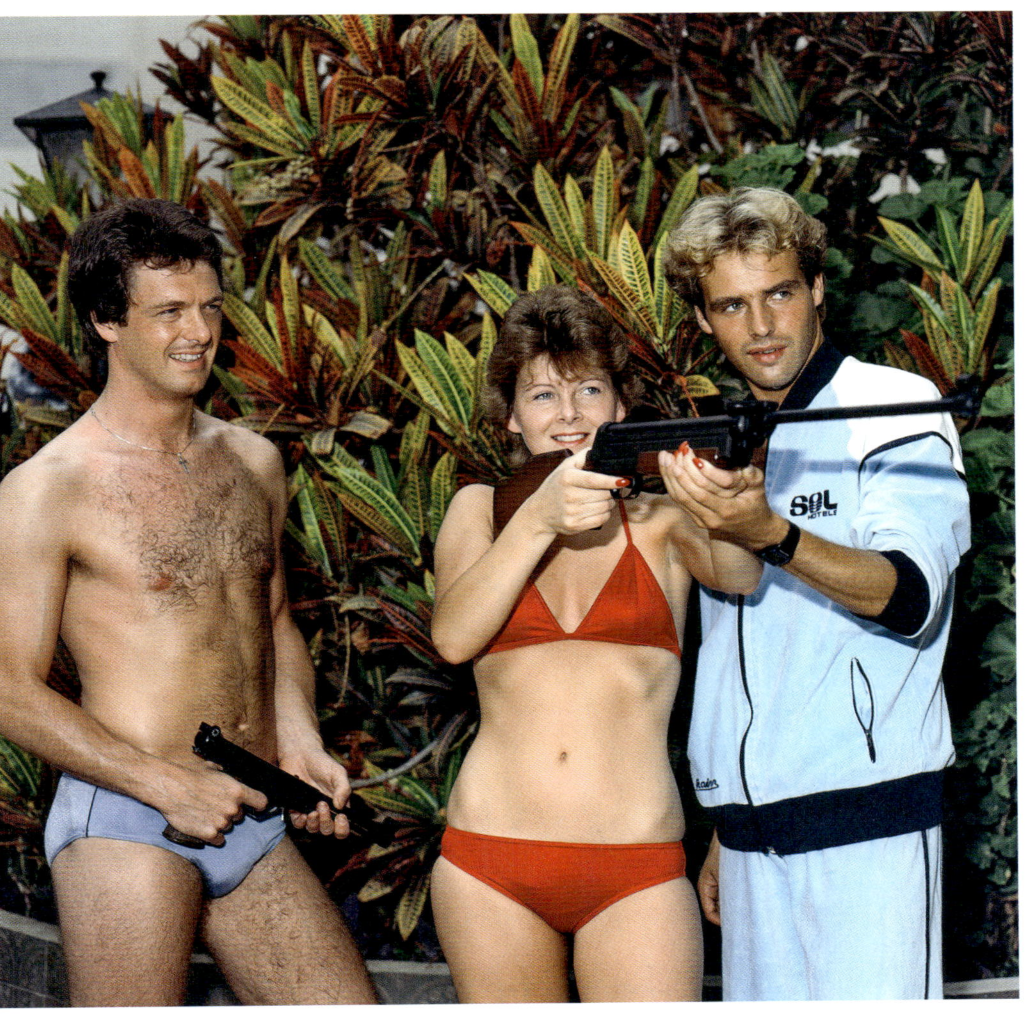
SOL
HOTELS

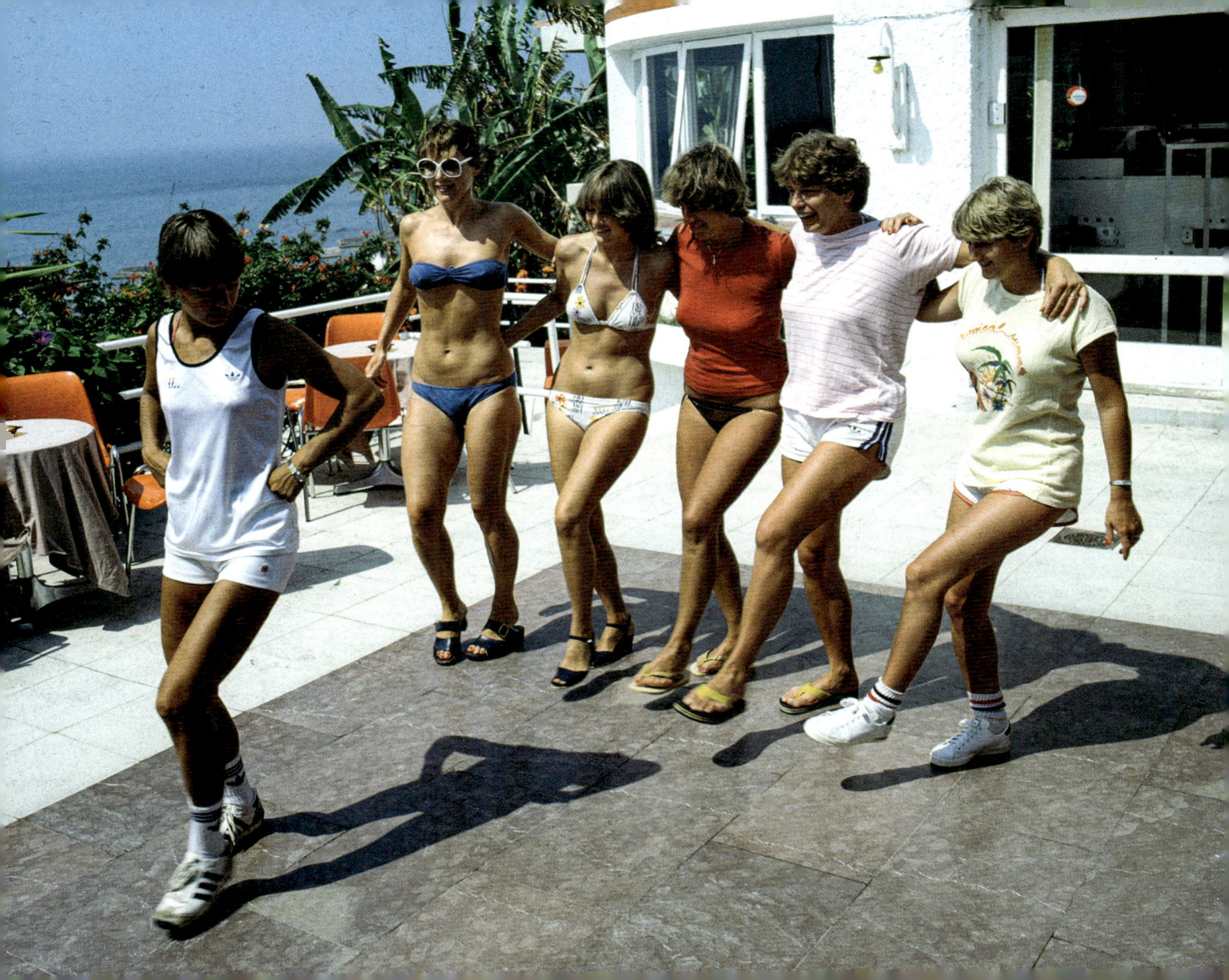

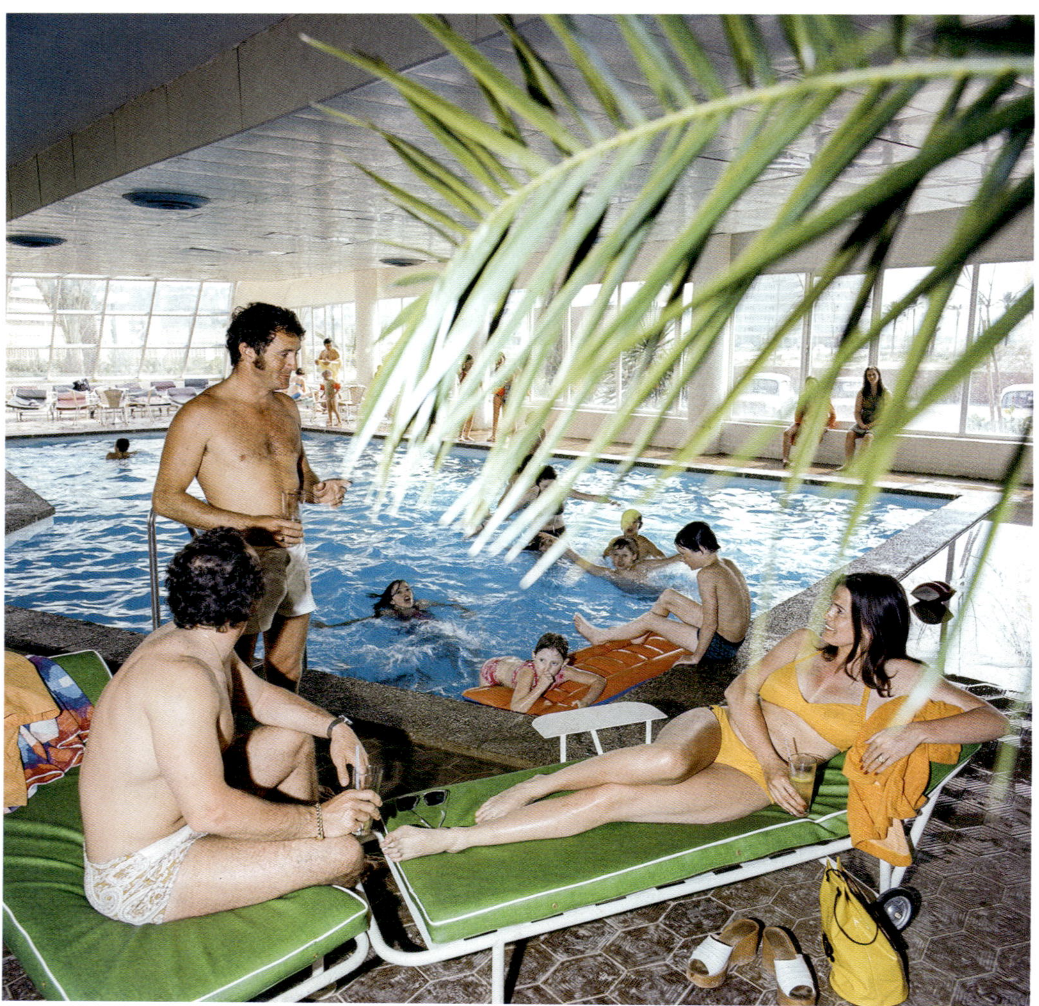

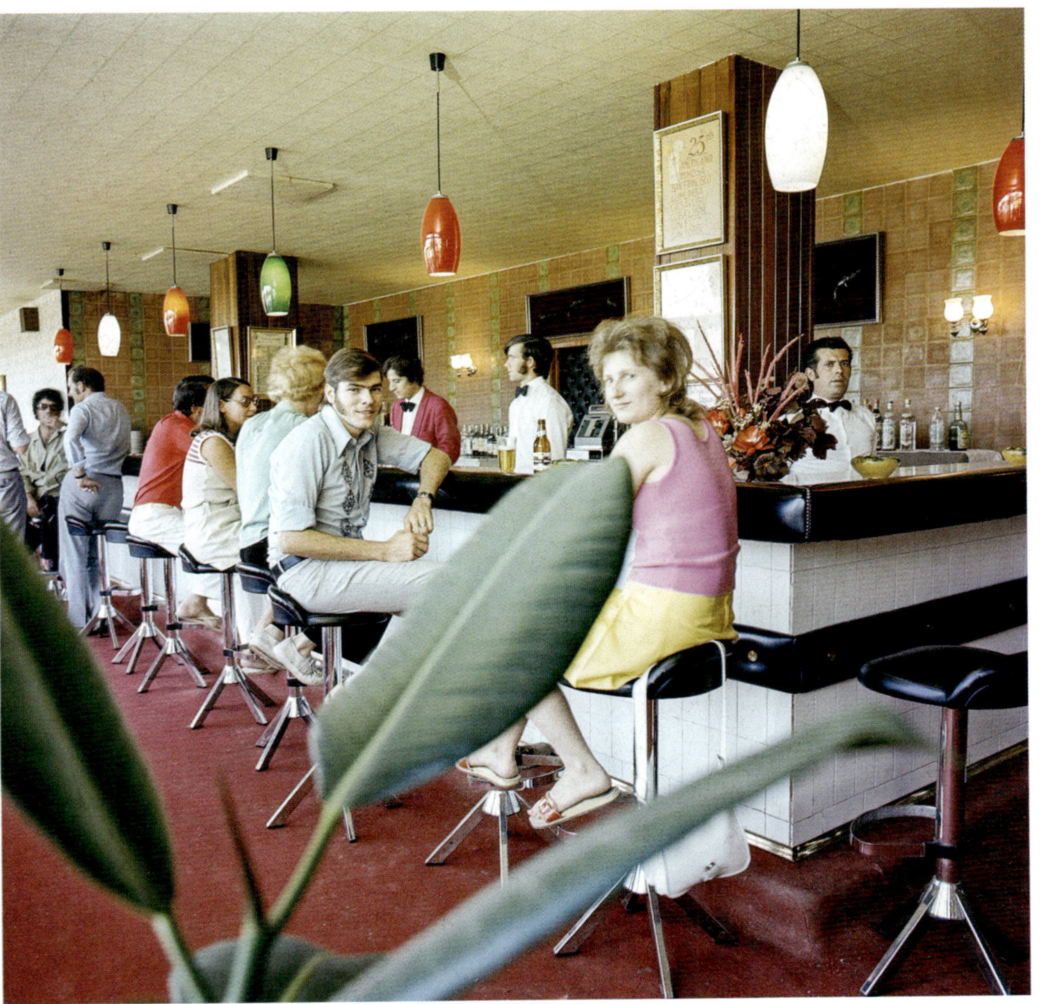

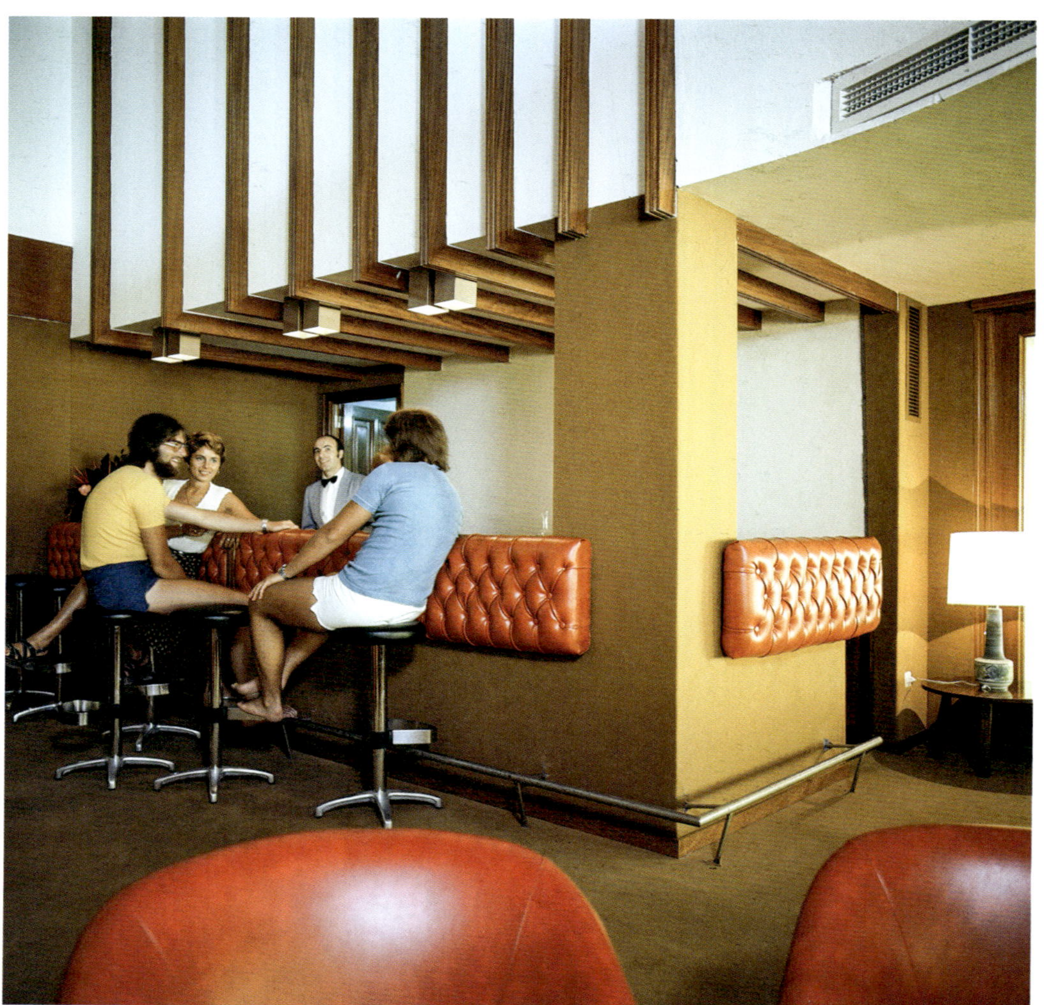

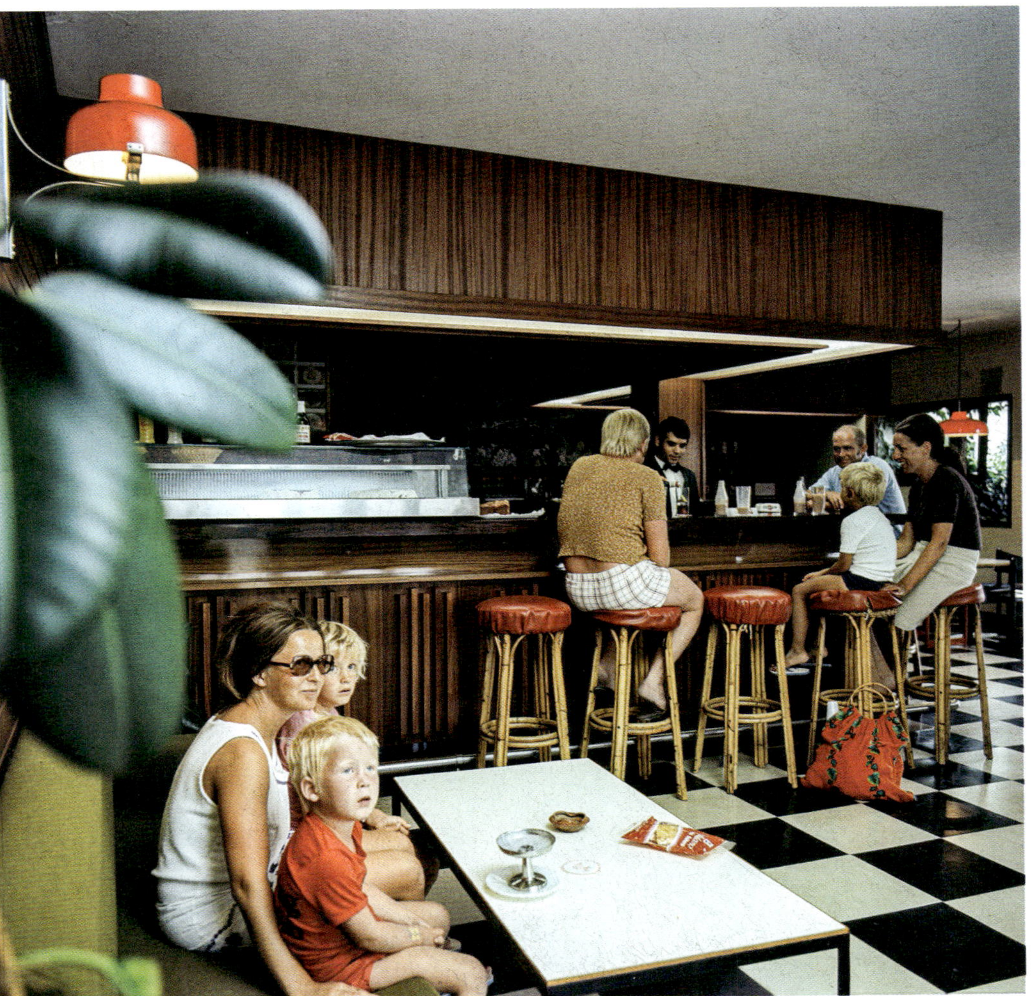

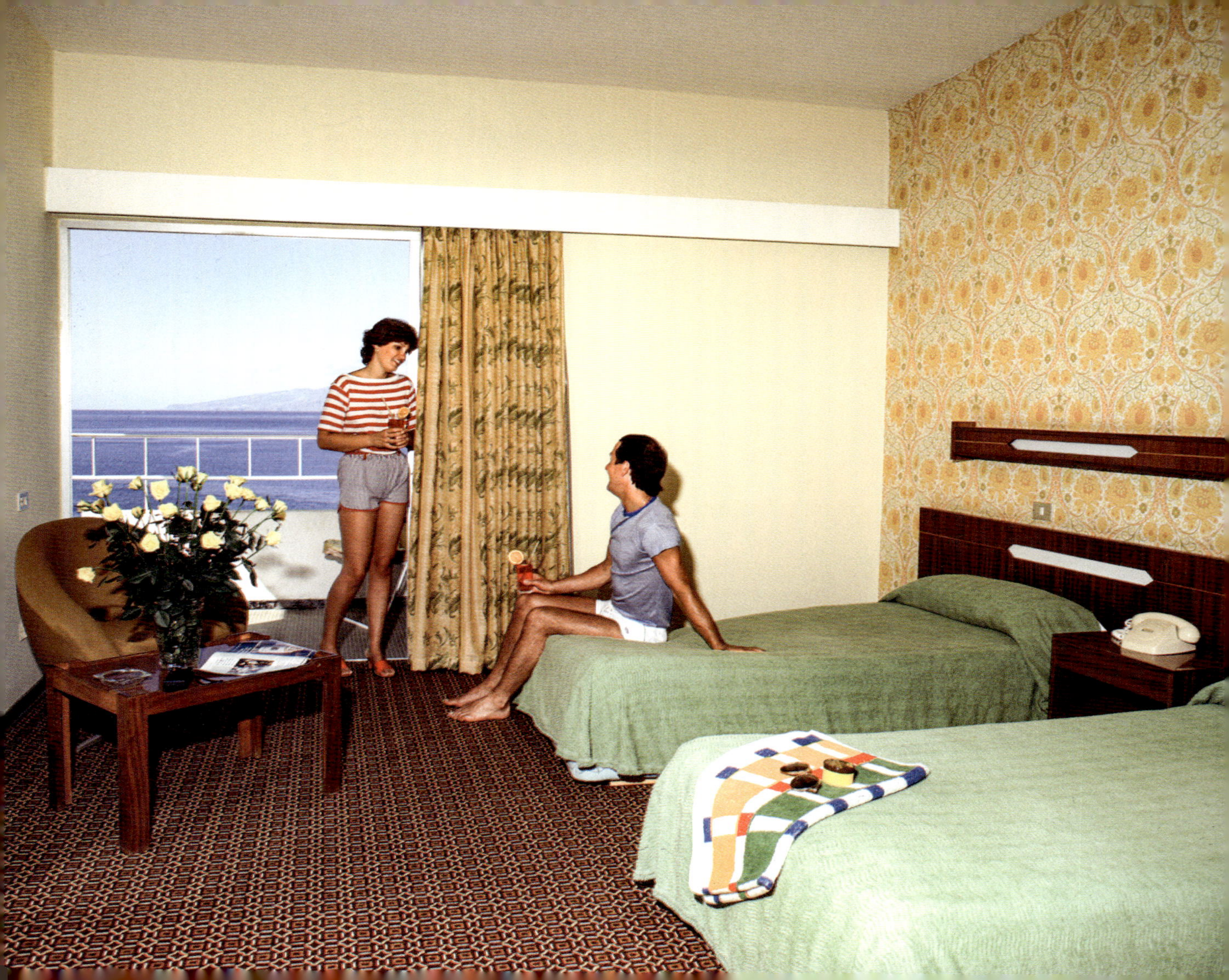

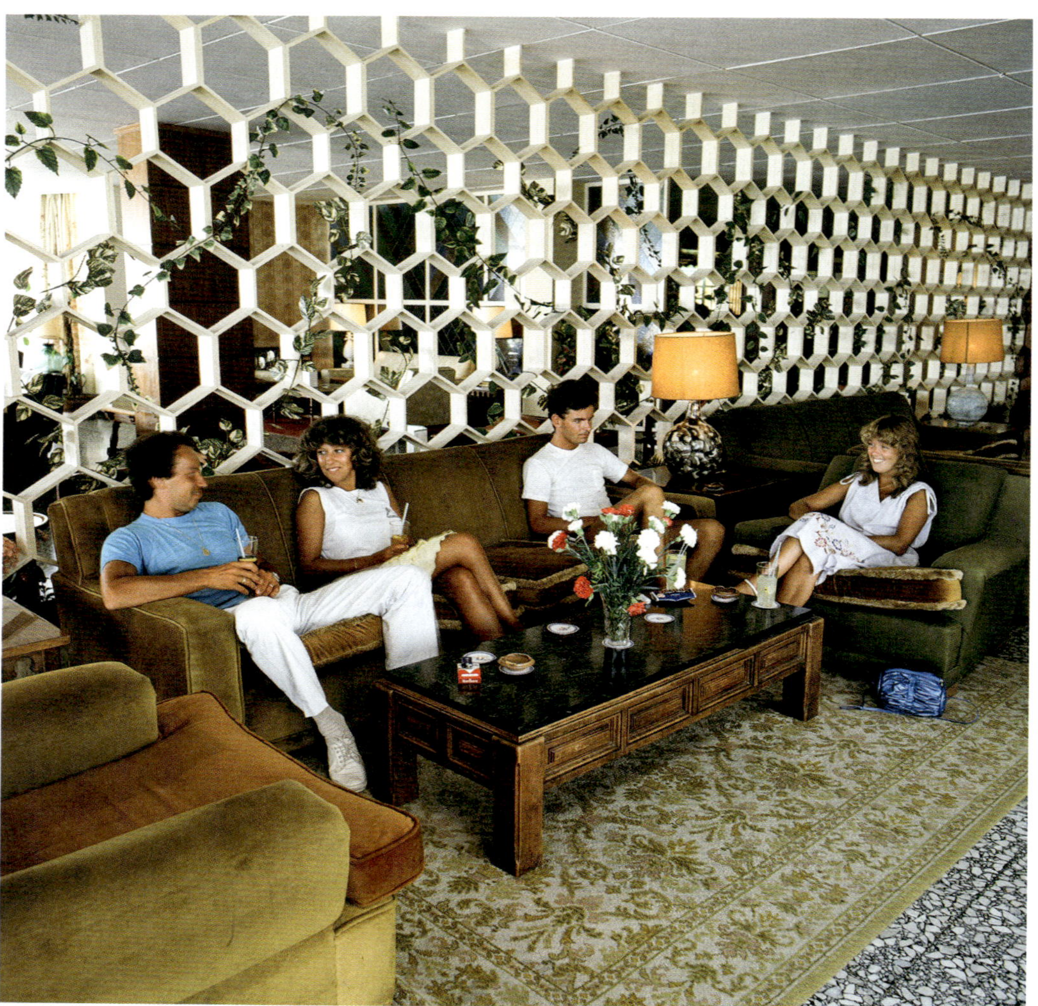

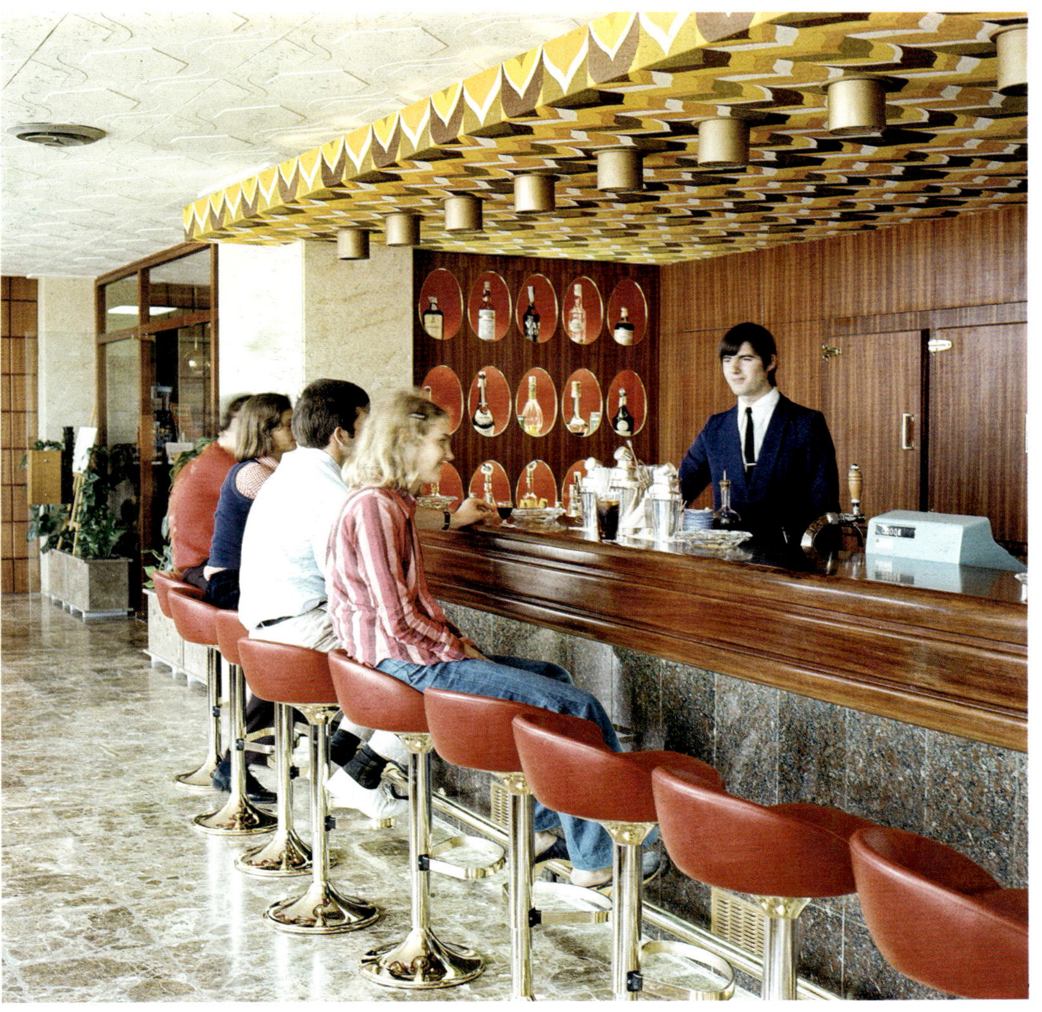

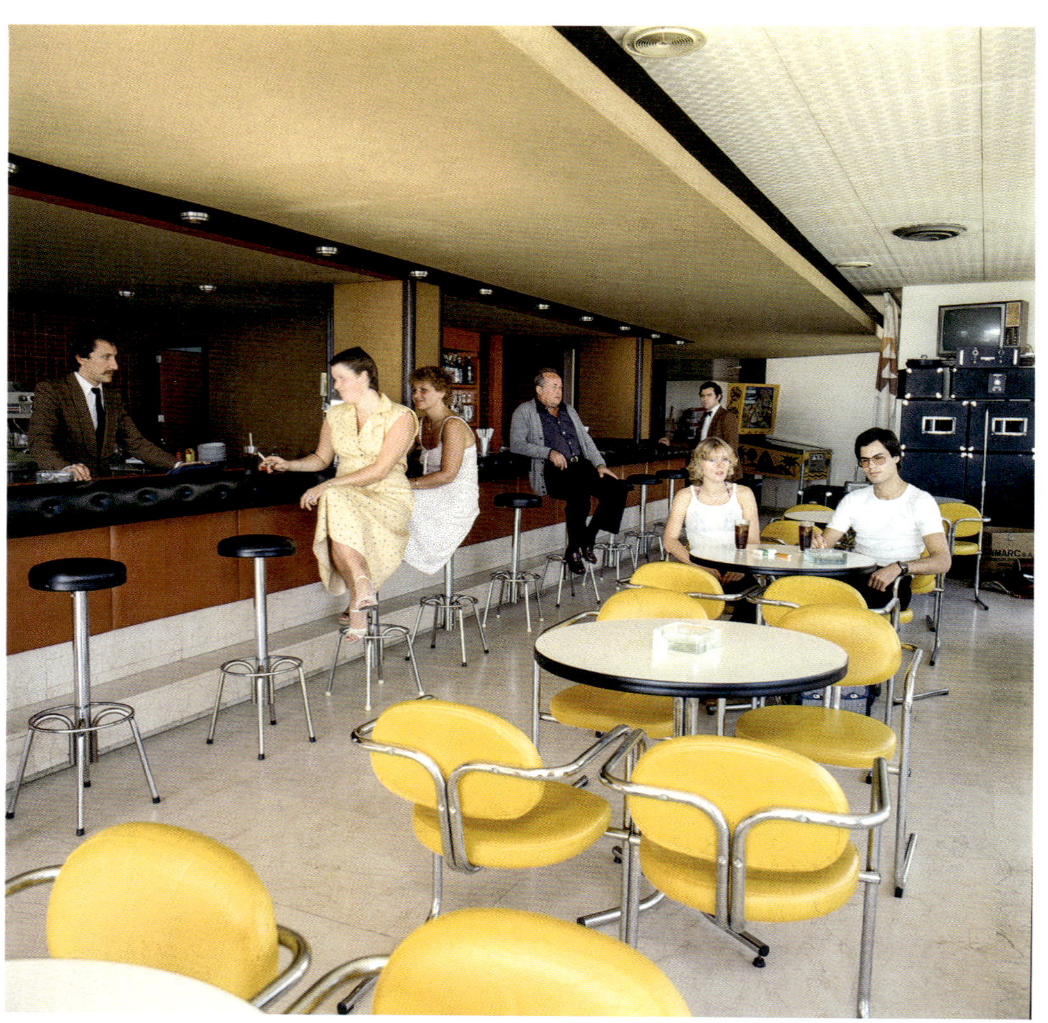

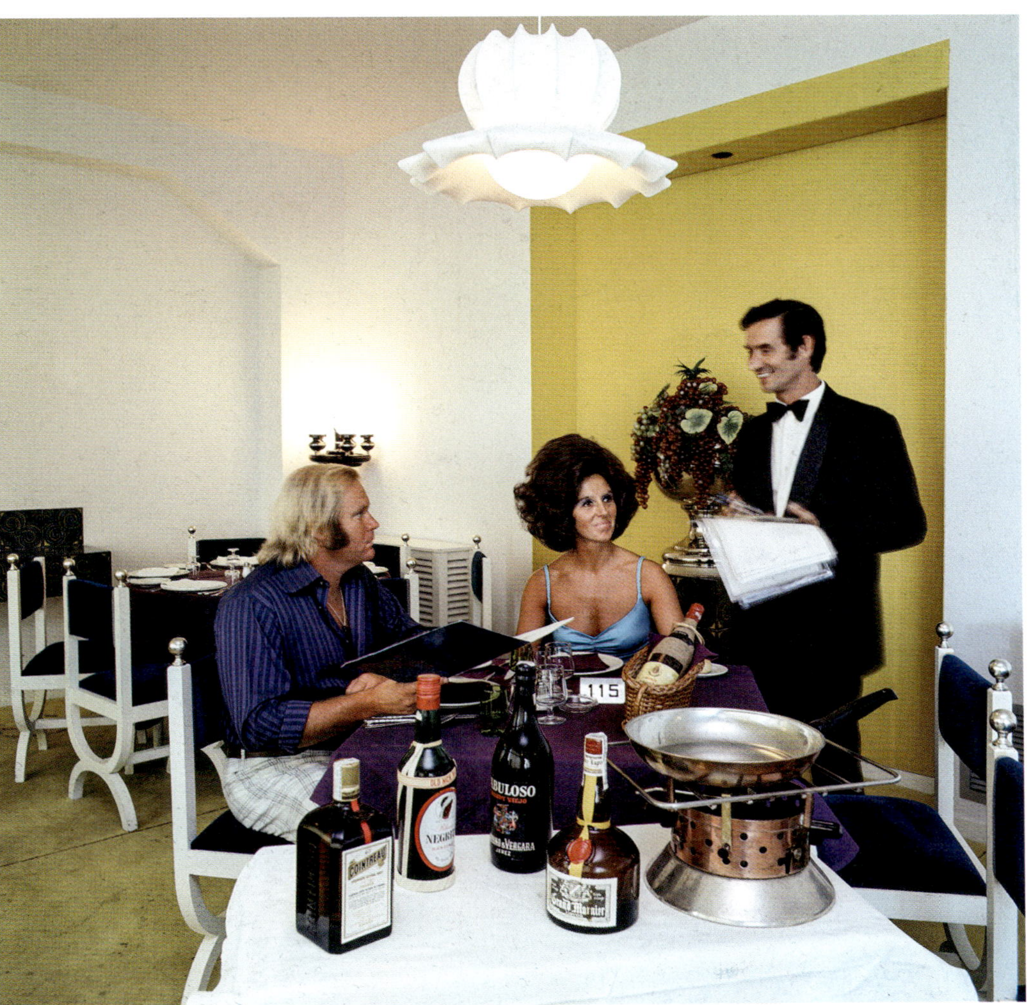
115
COINTREAU
NEGRITA
FABULOSO
CARLOS & VERGARA
Grand Marnier

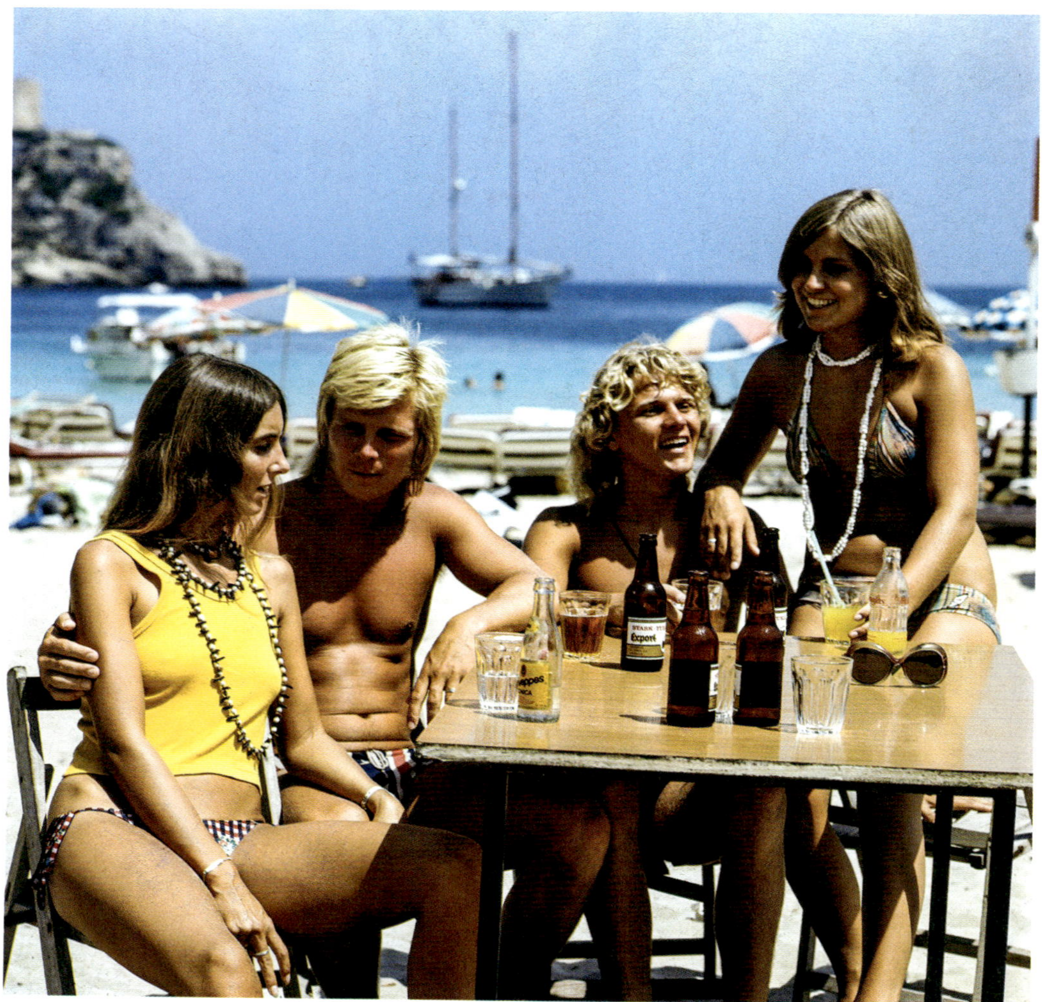

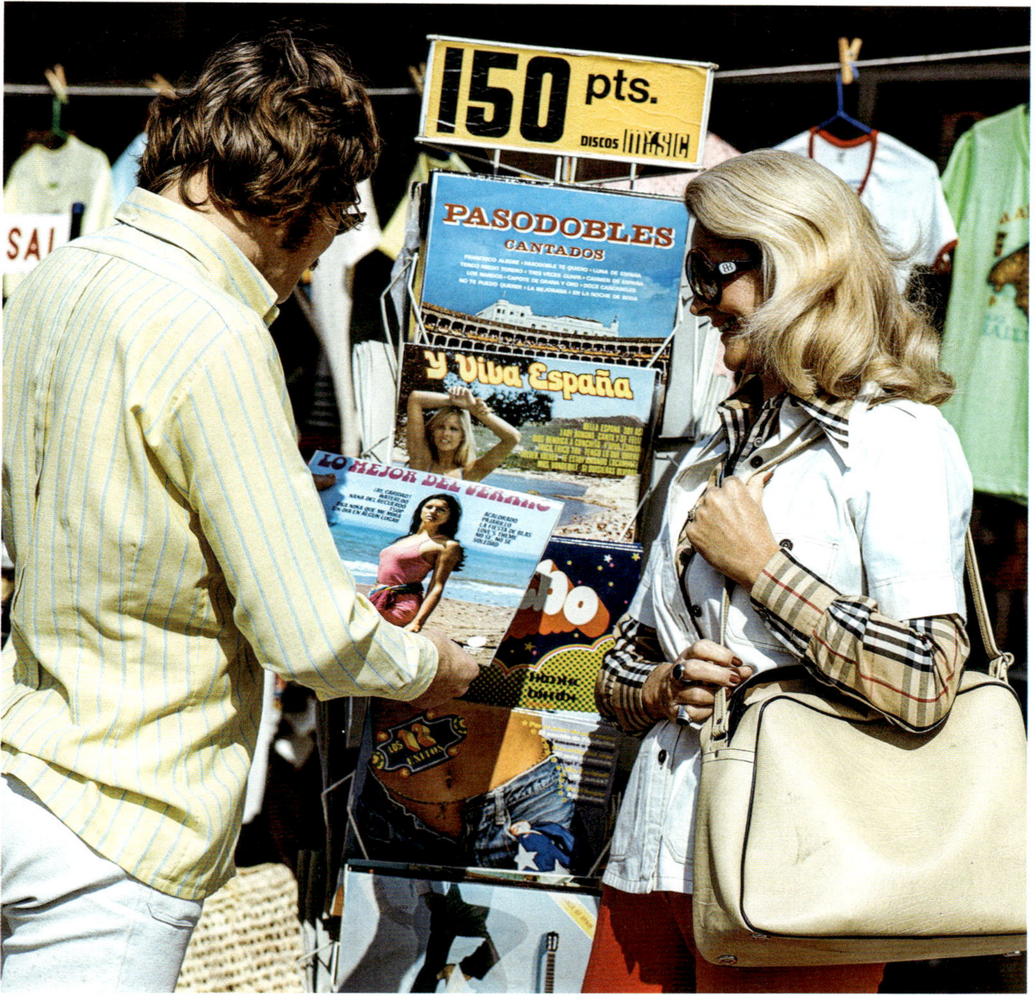

150 pts.
DISCOS MUSIC
PASODOBLES
CANTADOS
Y Viva España
LO MEJOR DEL VERANO

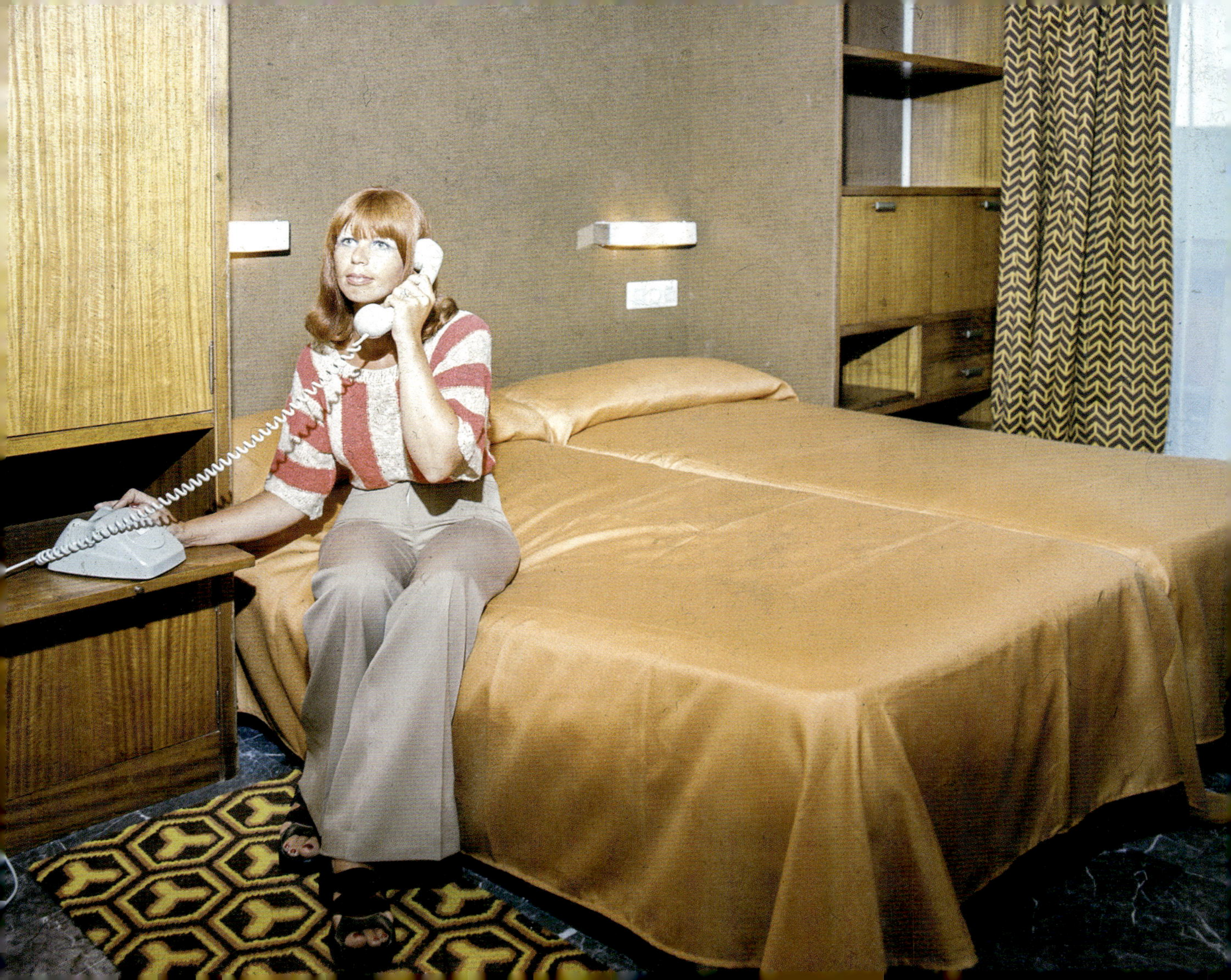

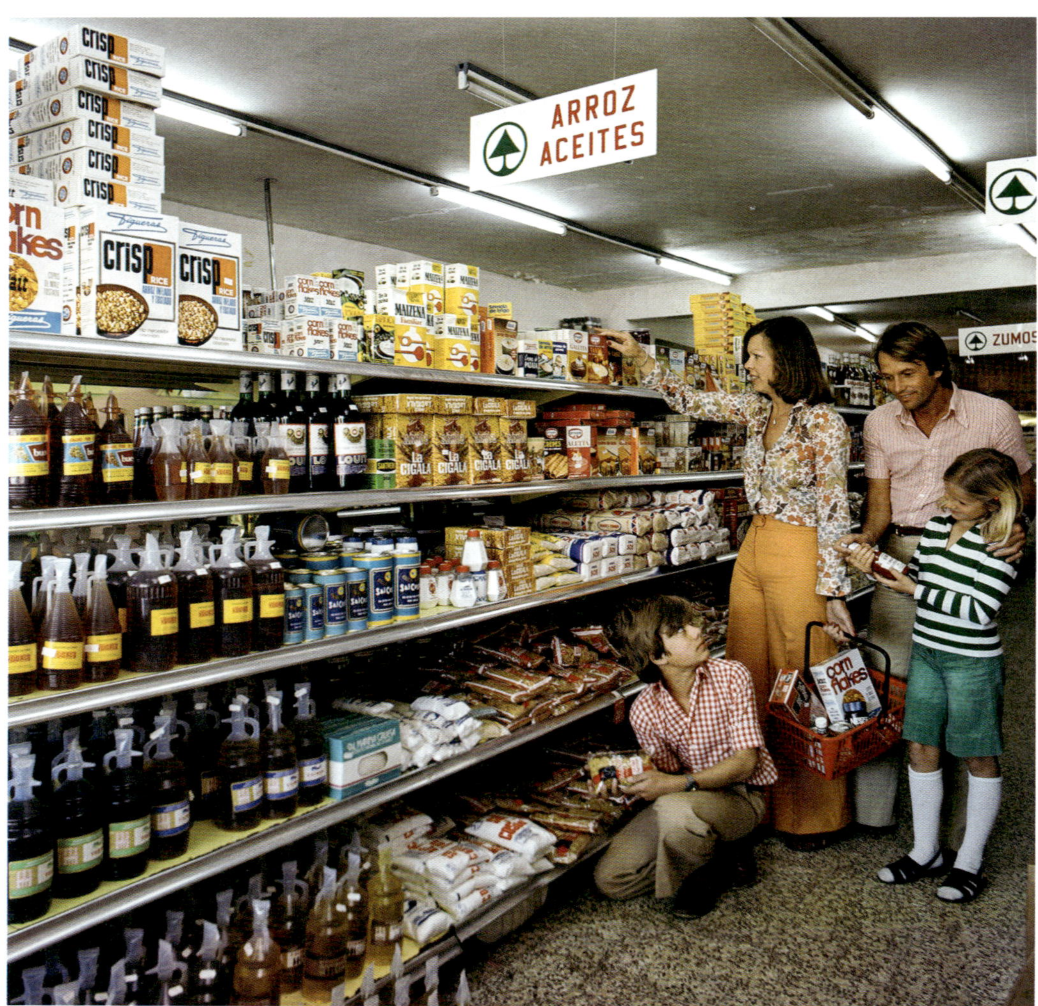

ARROZ
ACEITES
ZUMOS
crisp
crisp
crisp
crisp
crisp
corn flakes
crisp RICE
crisp RICE
MAIZENA
La CIGALA
corn flakes

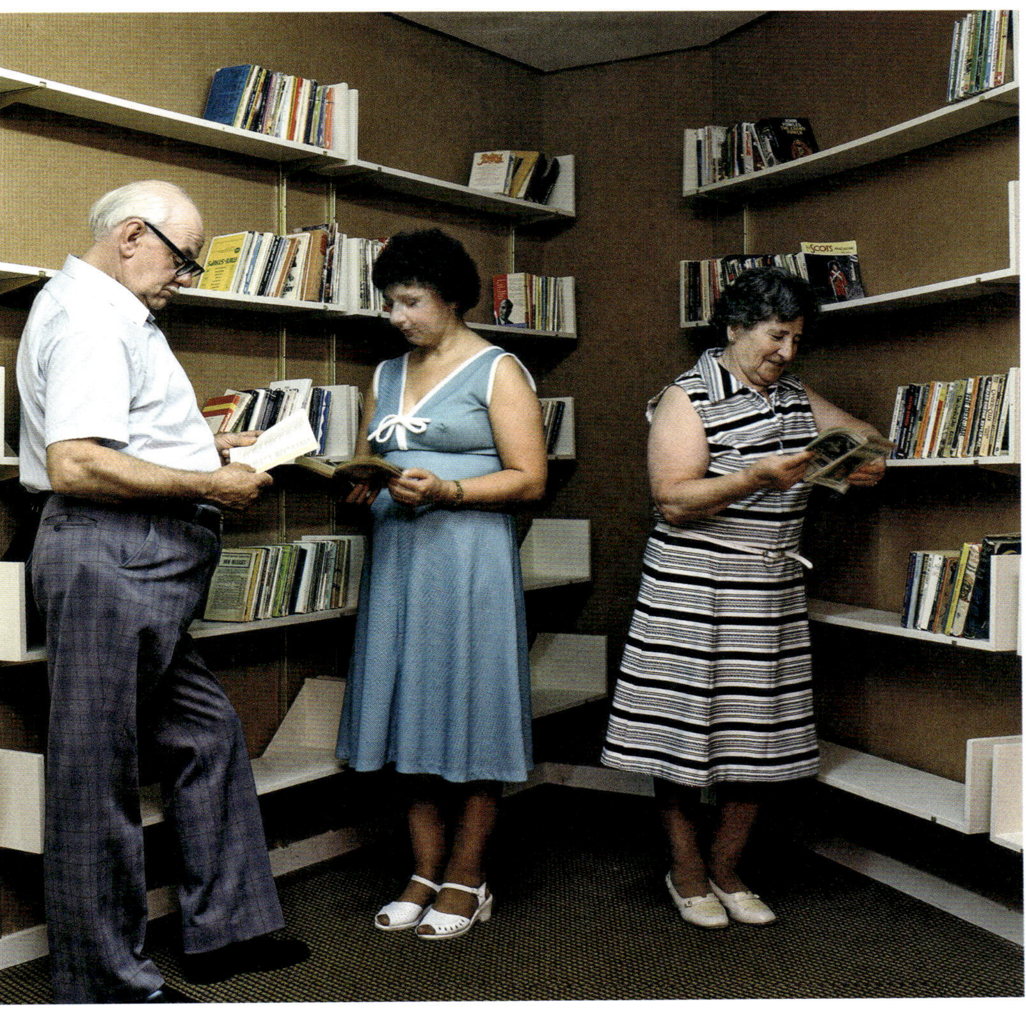

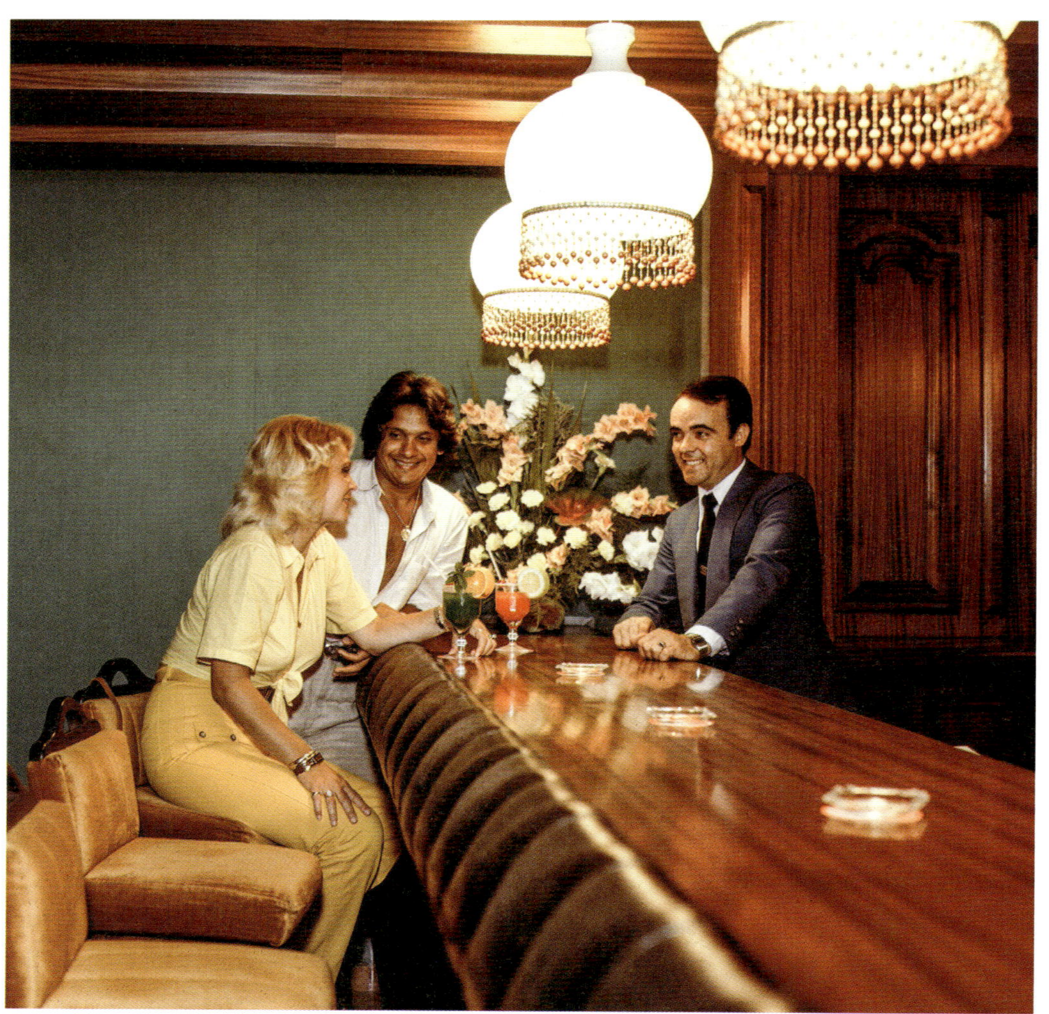

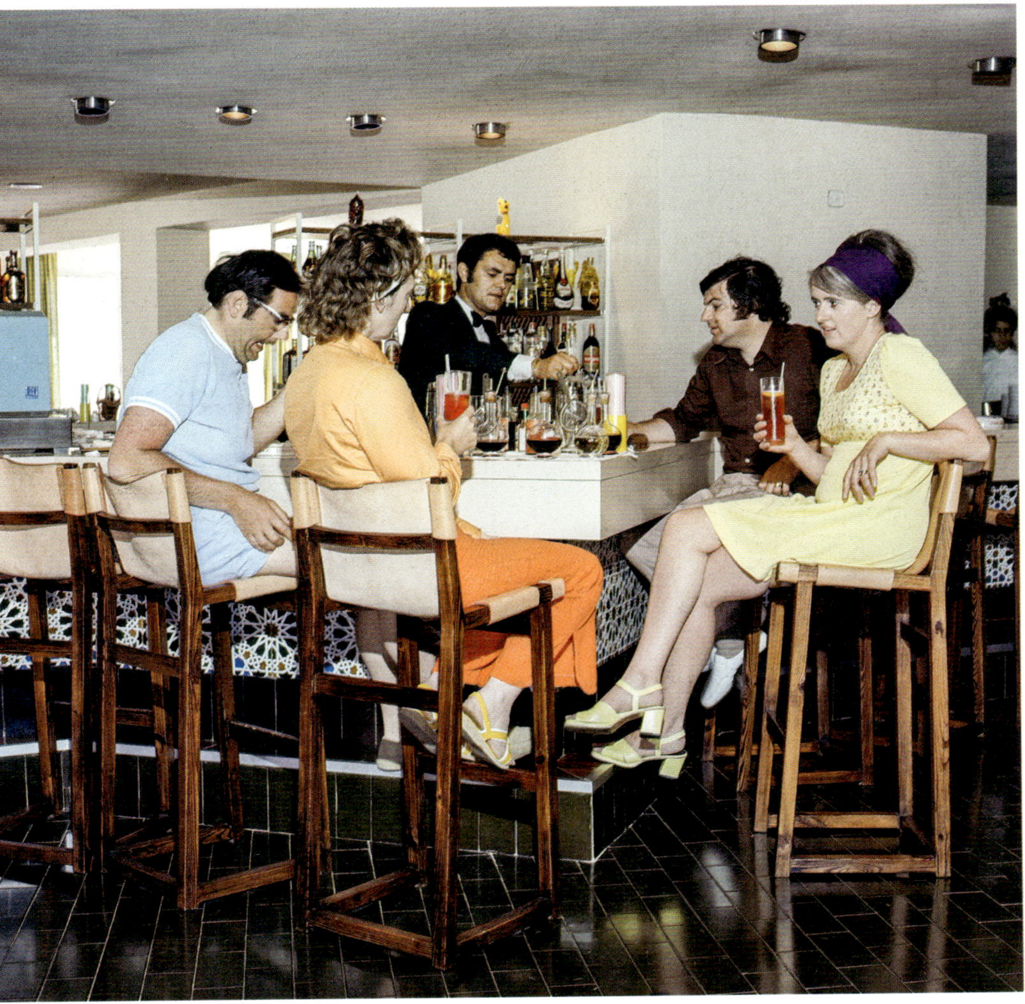

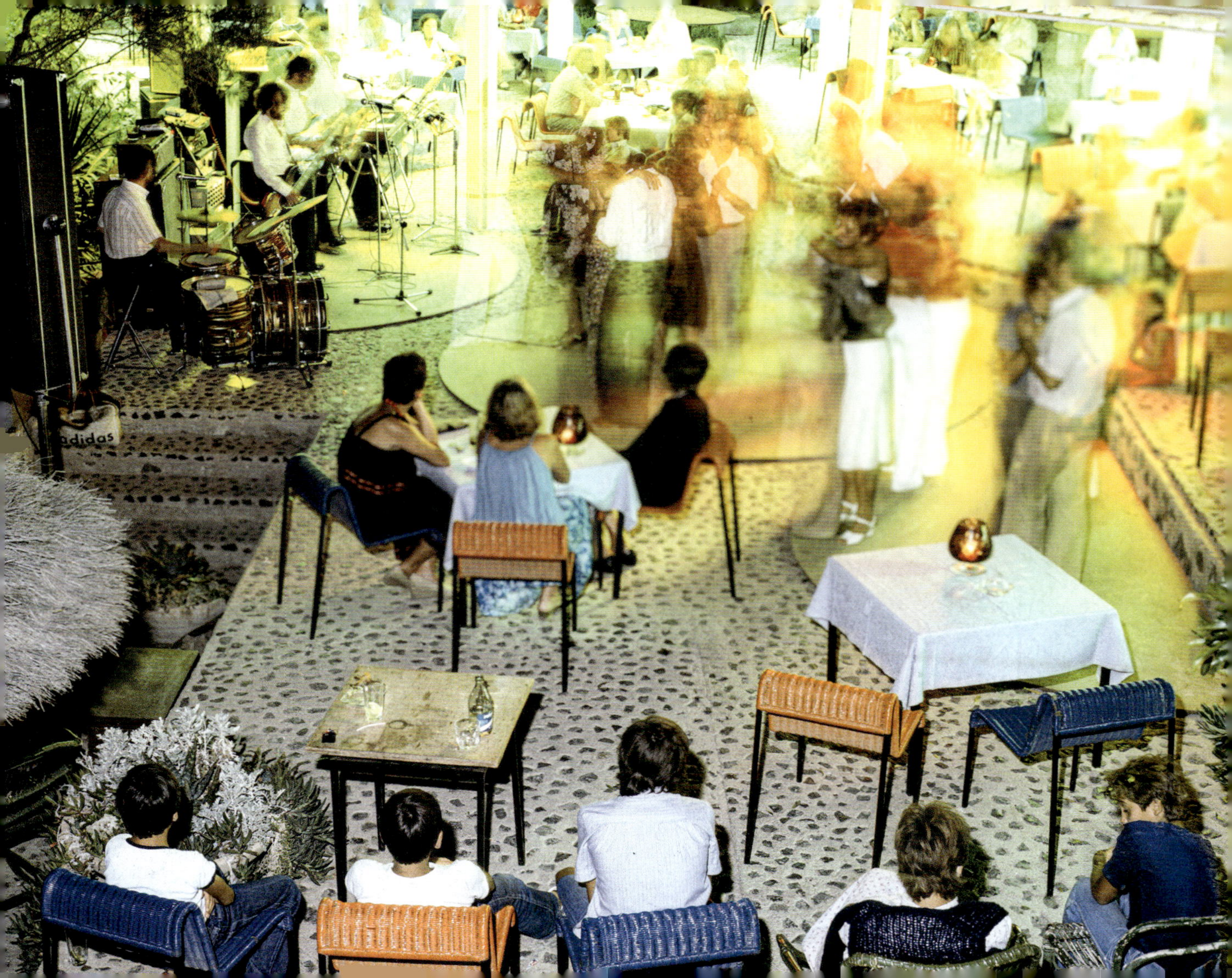

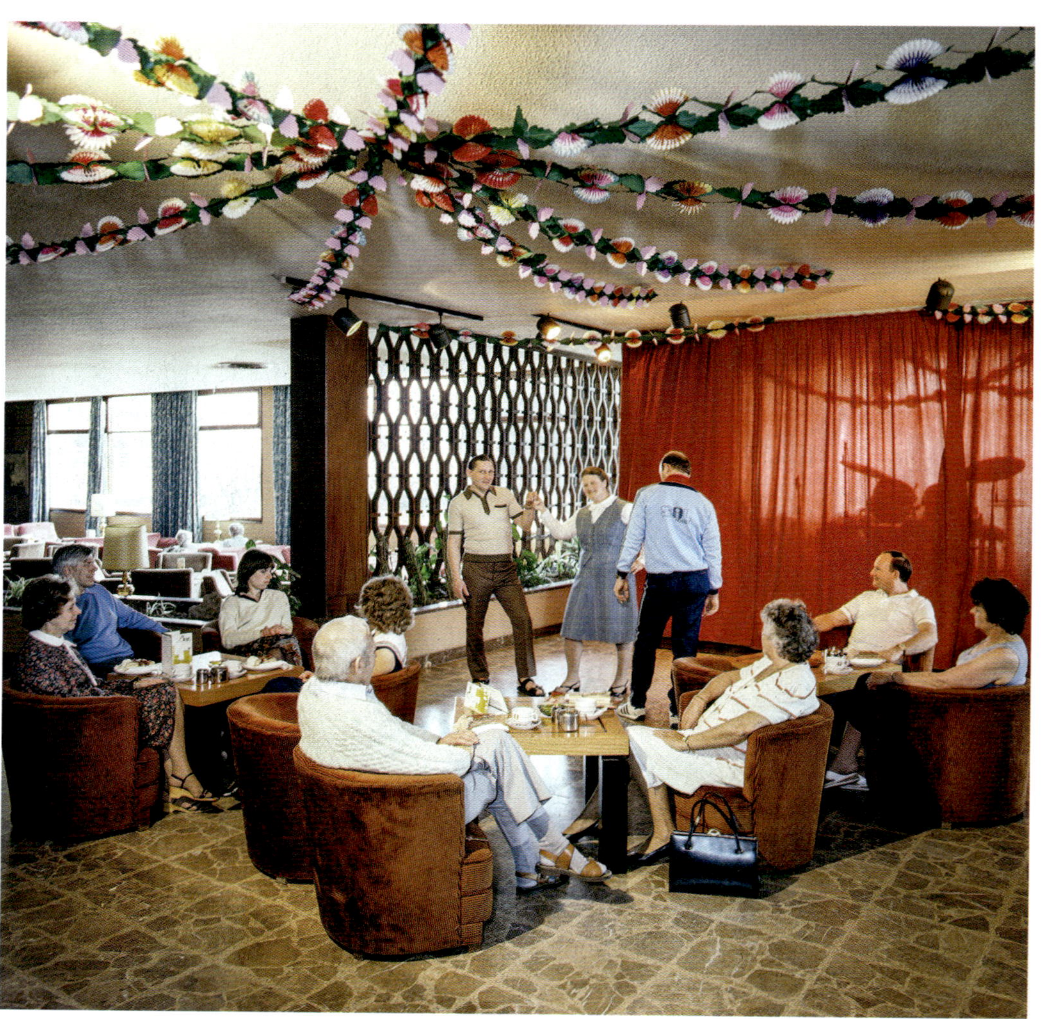

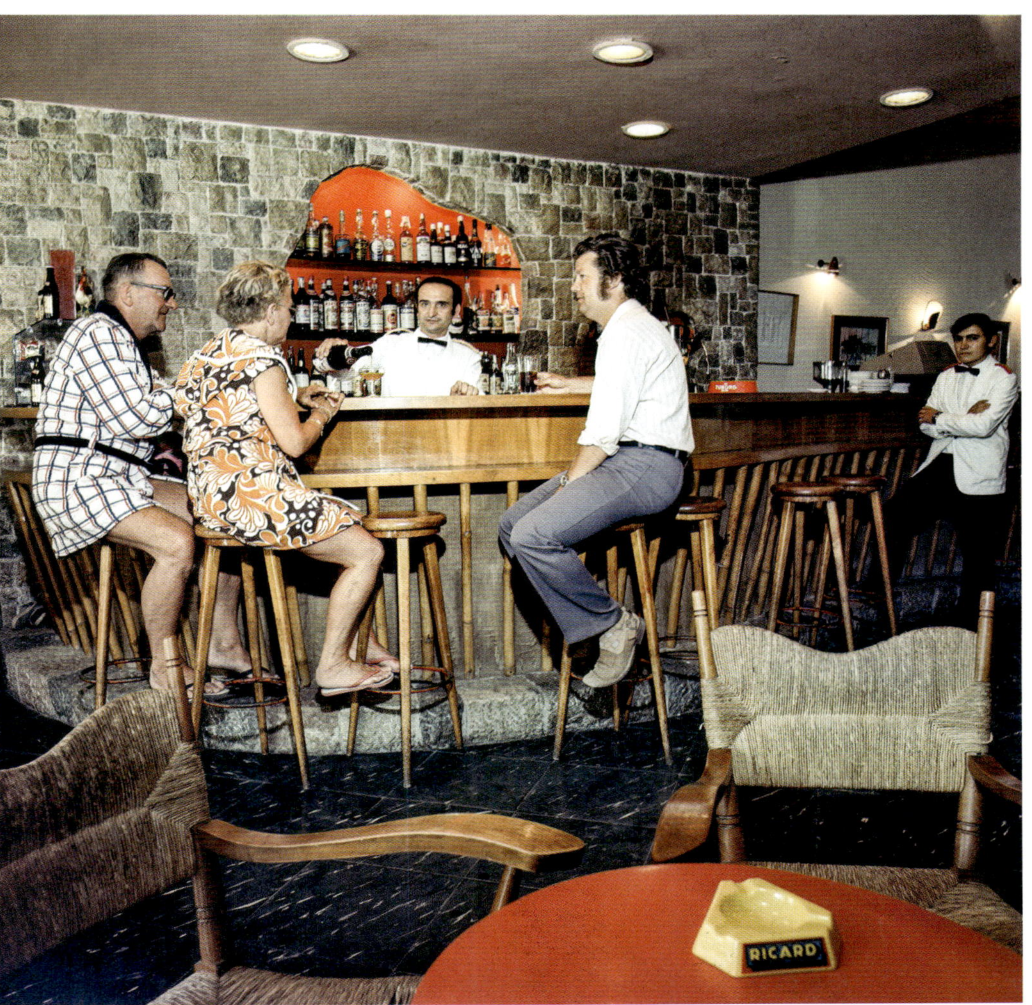
RICARD

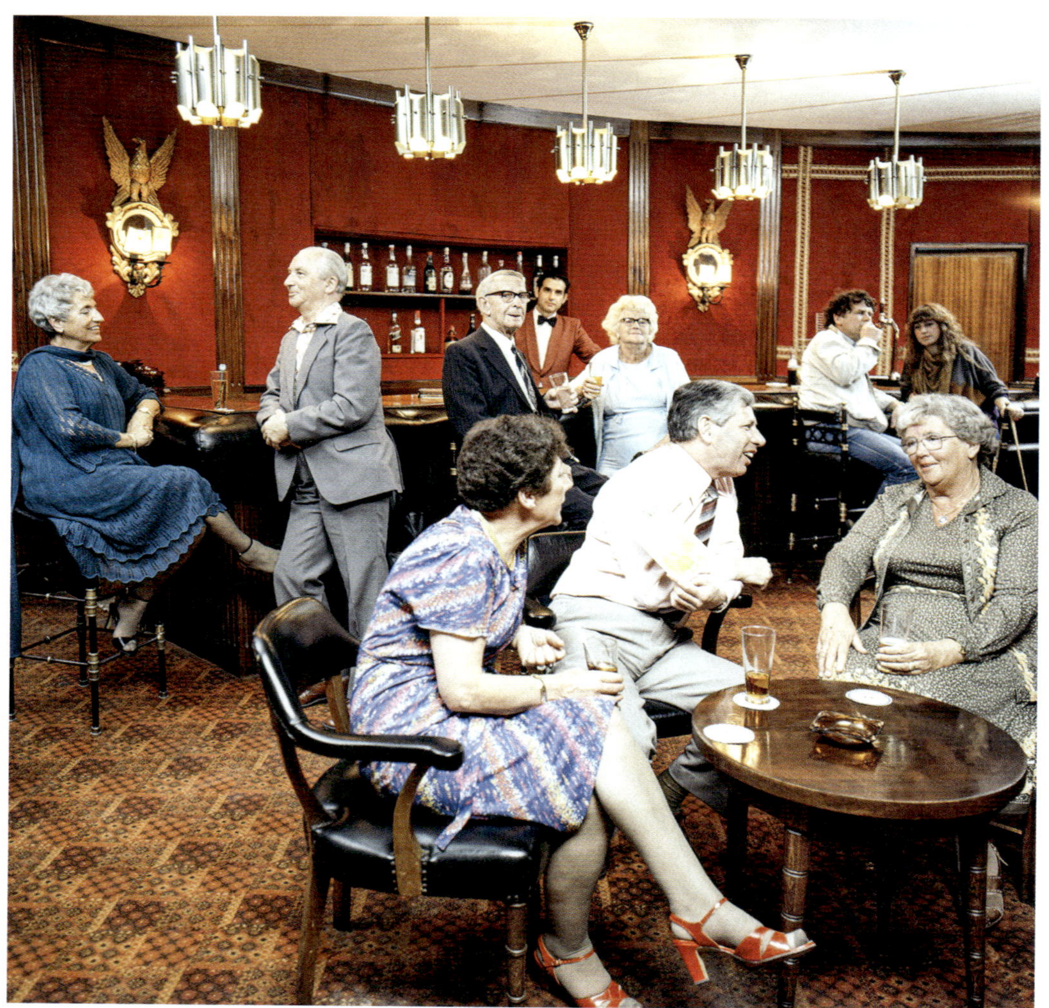

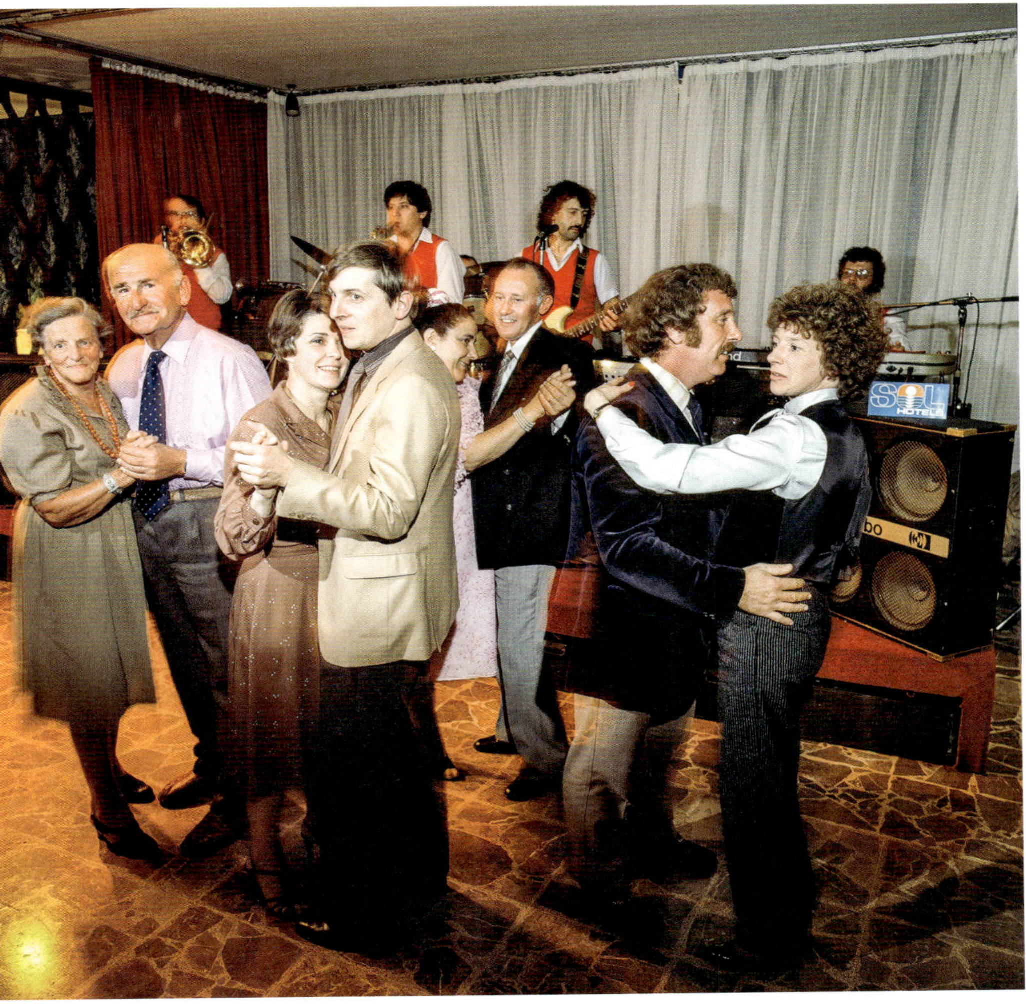

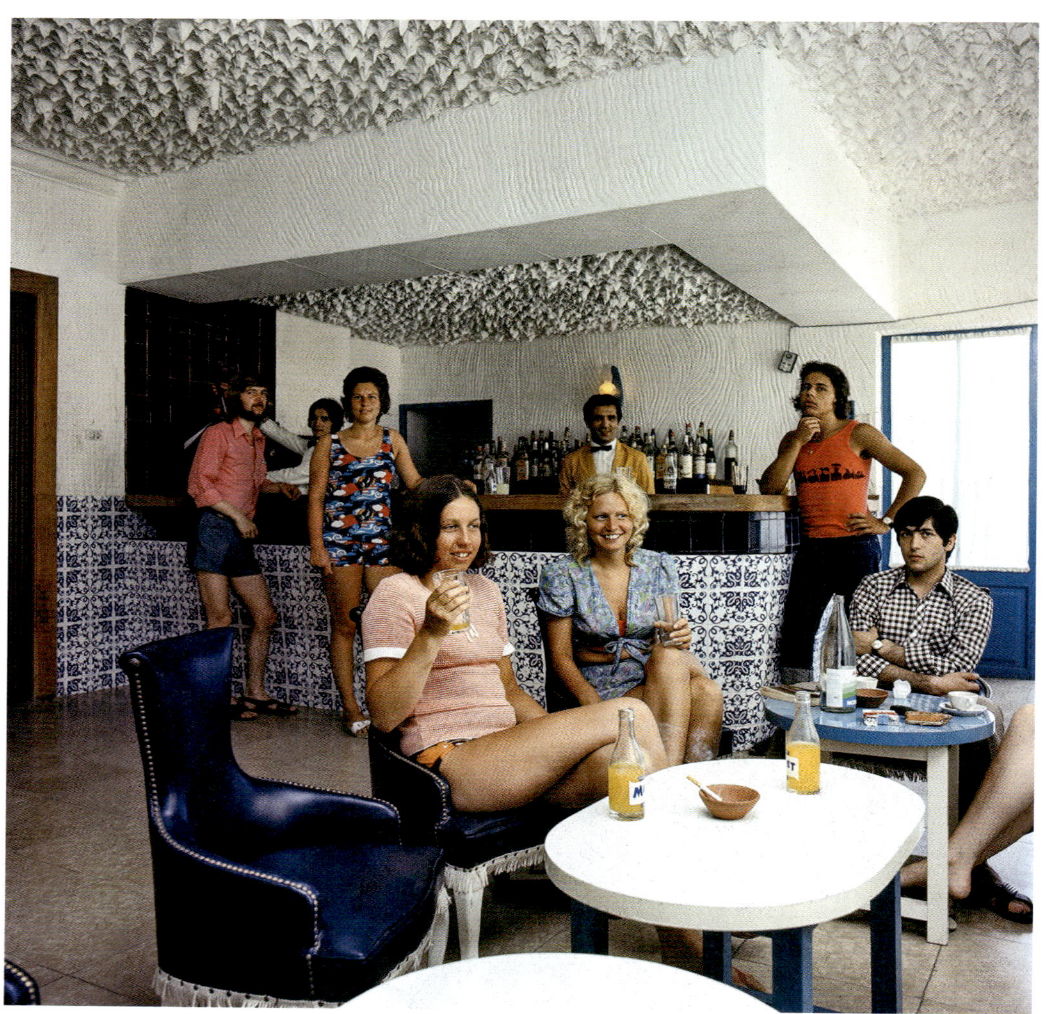

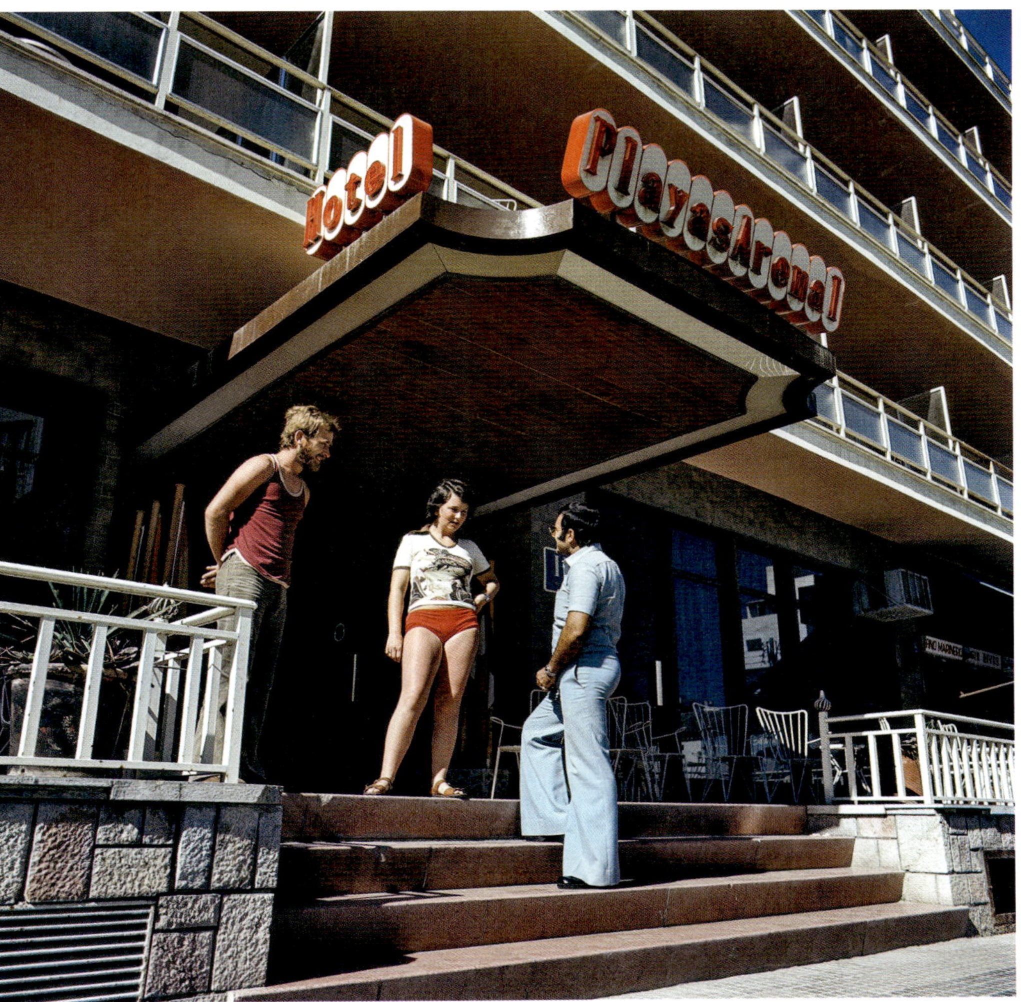
Hotel
Playas Arenal

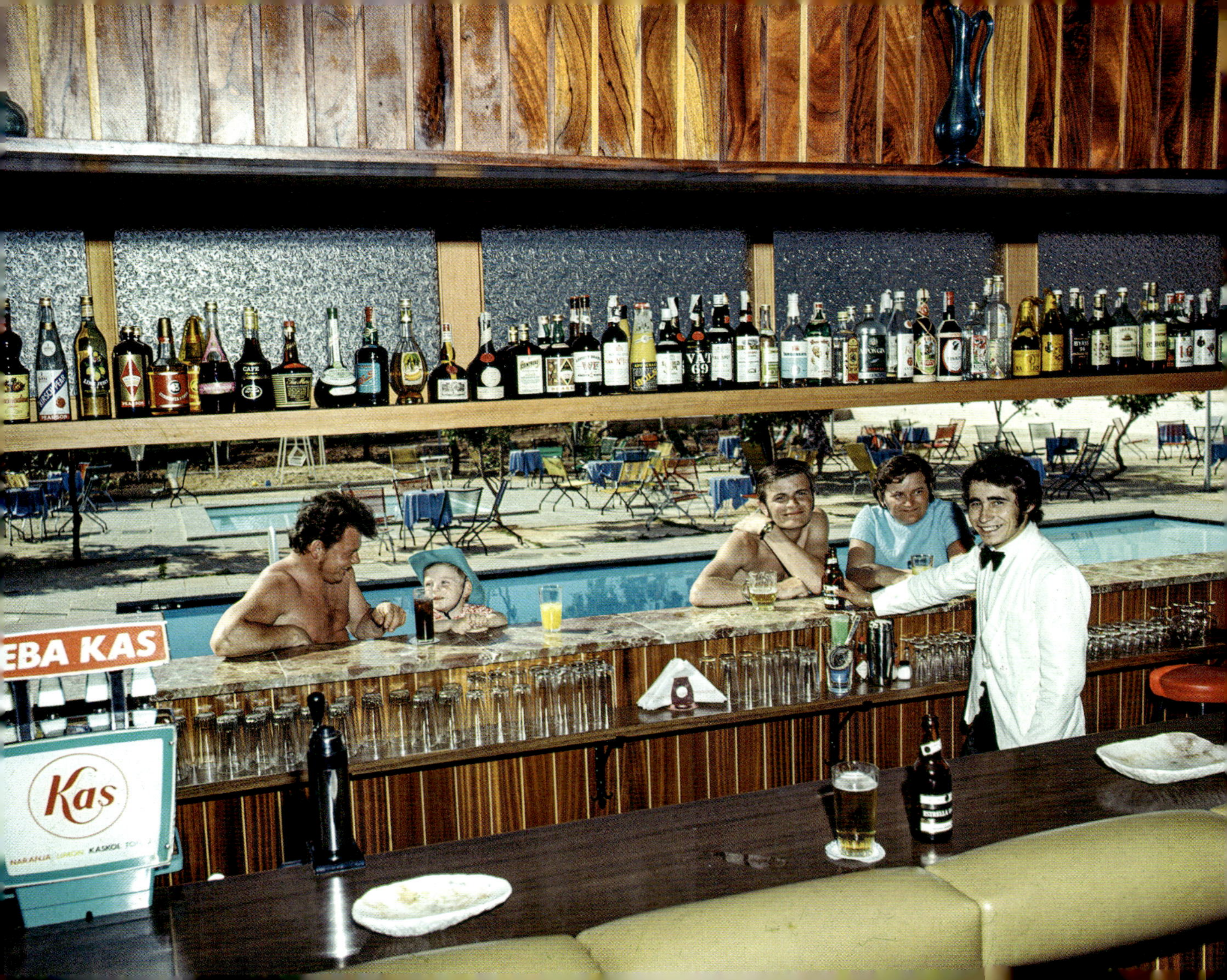
EBA KAS
Kas
NARANJA LIMON KASKOL TON

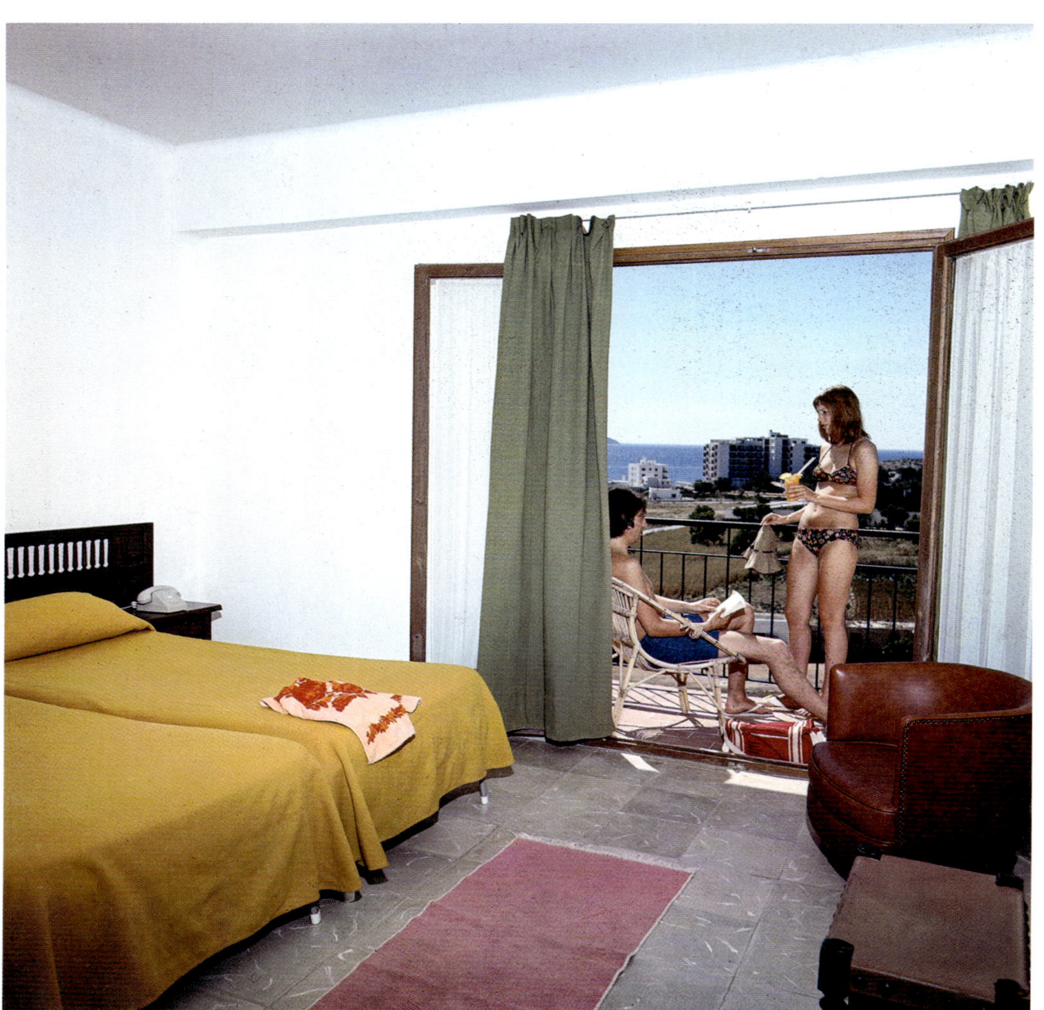

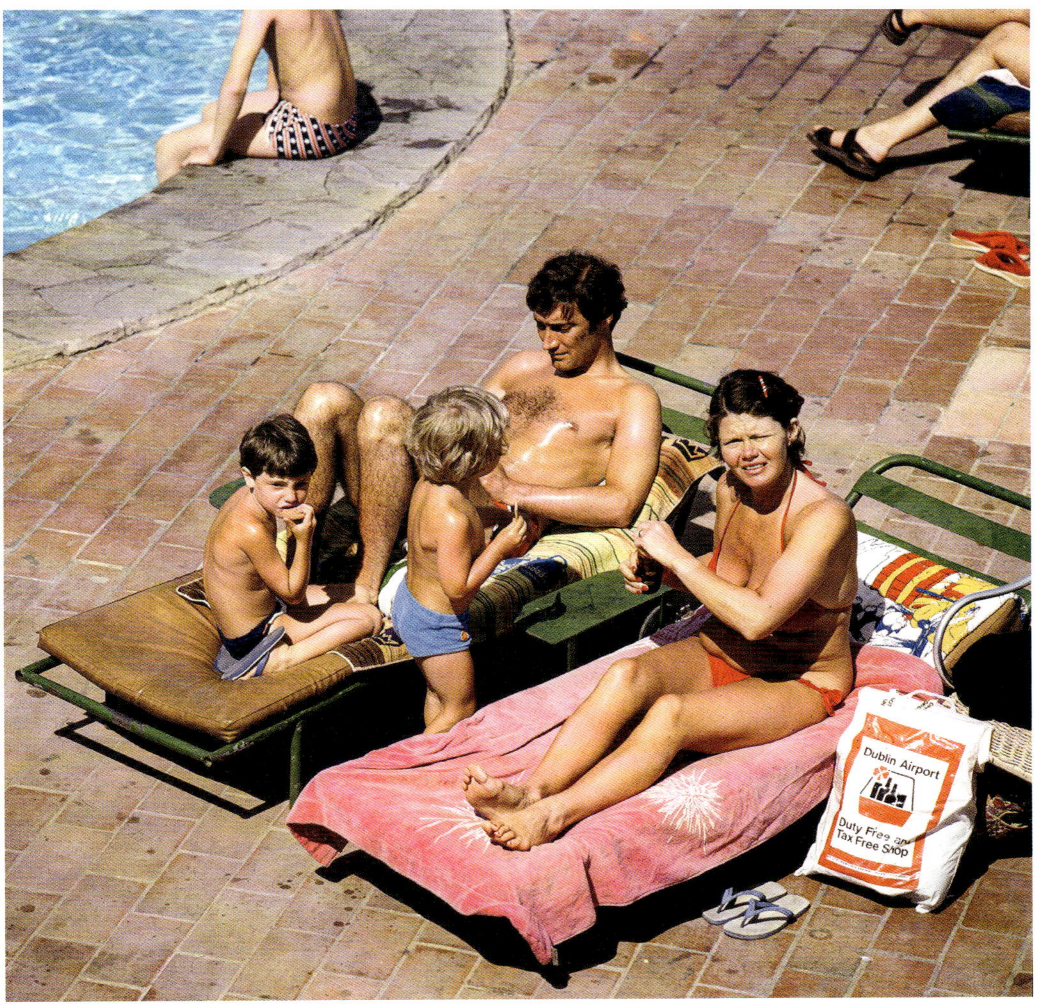
Dublin Airport
Duty Free and
Tax Free Shop

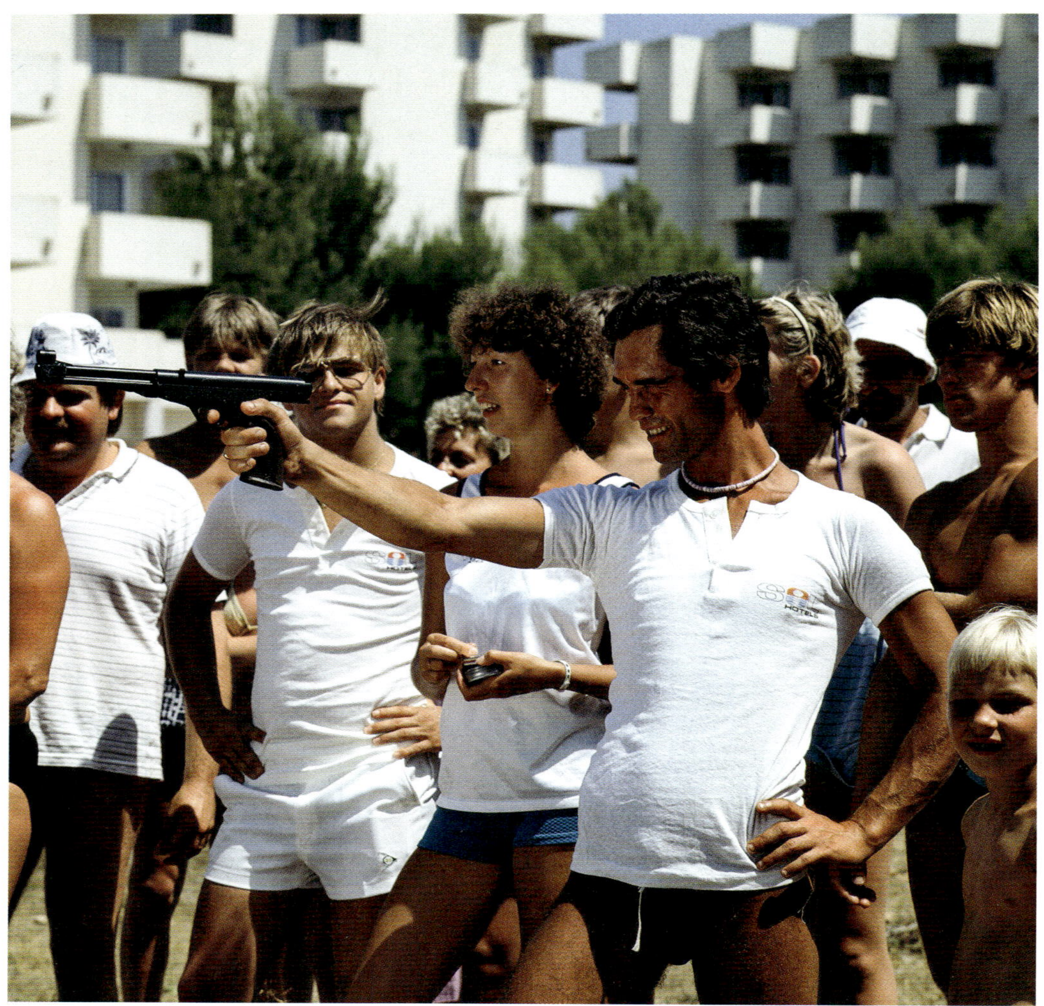

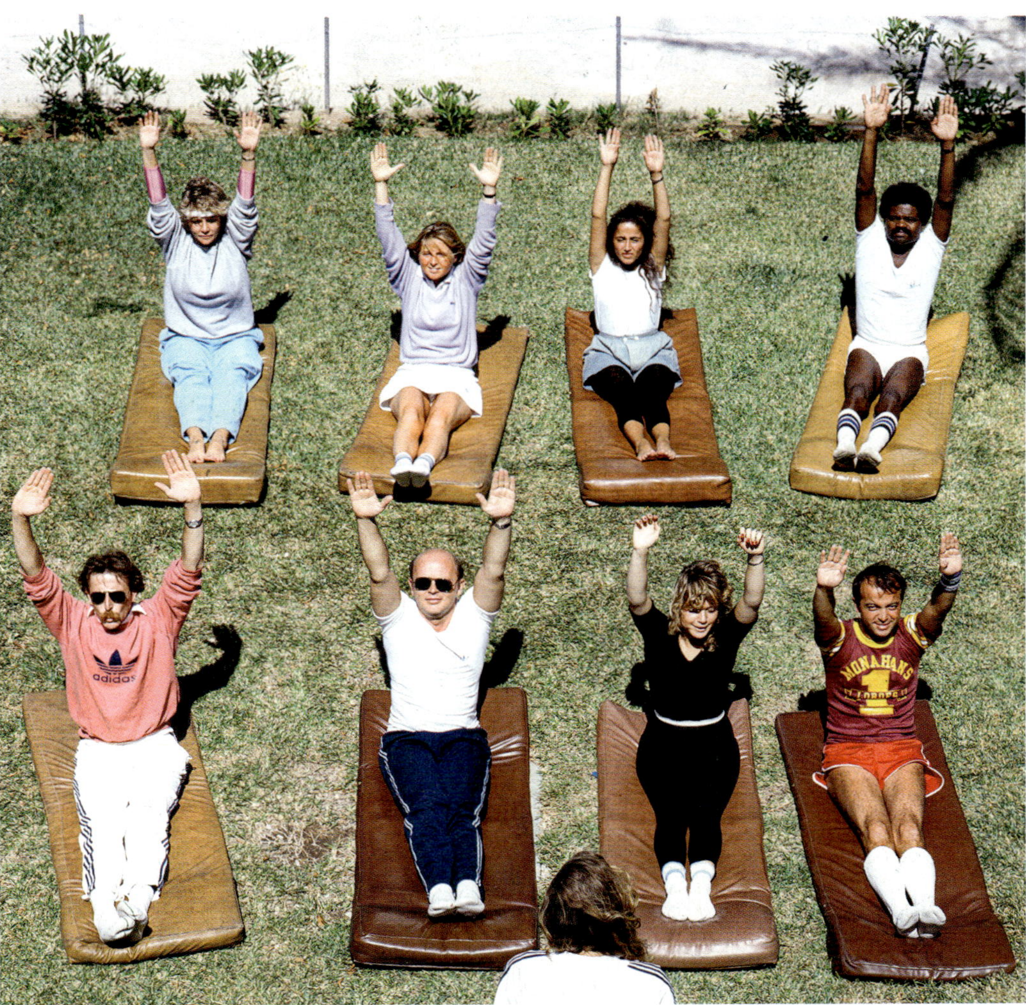

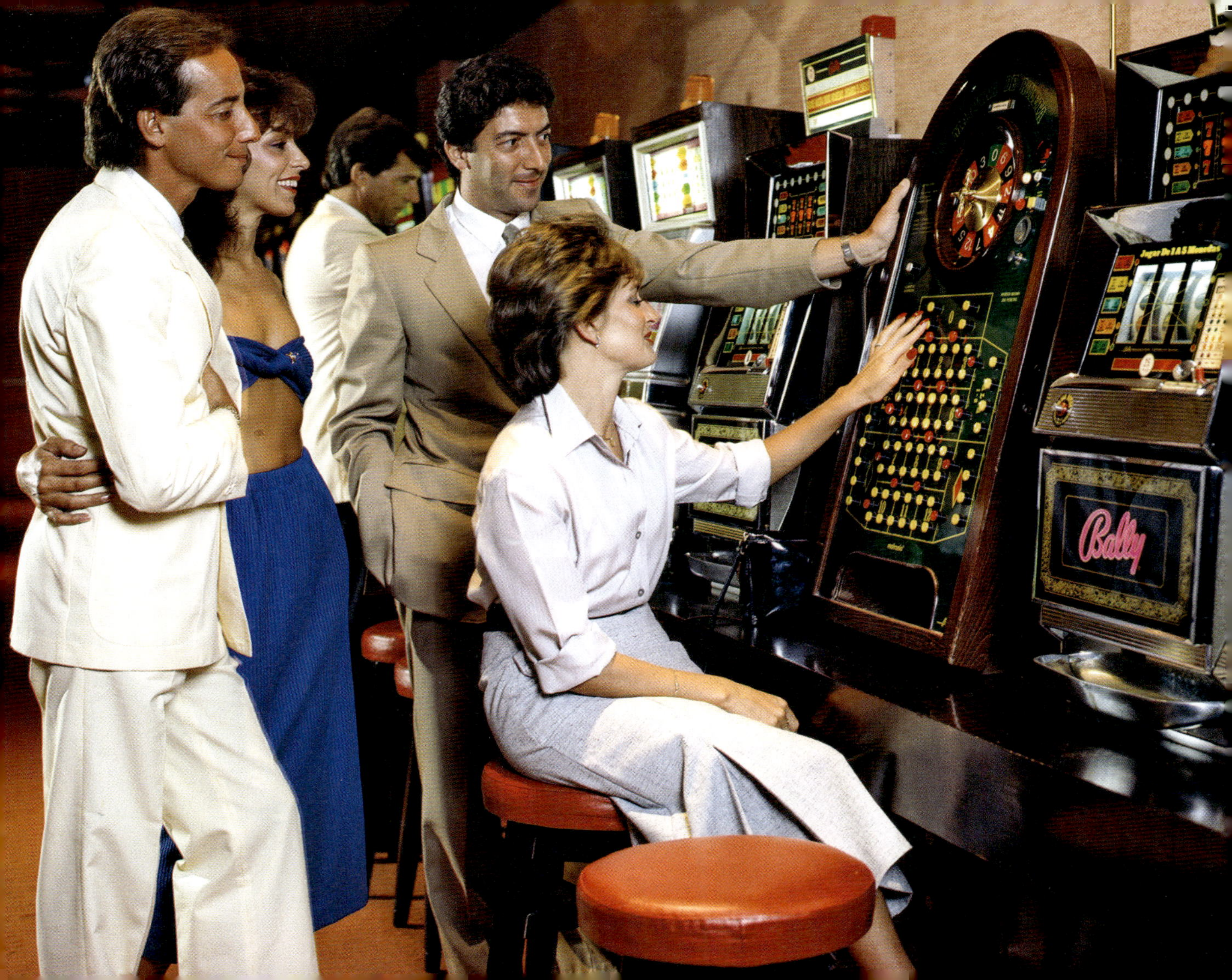

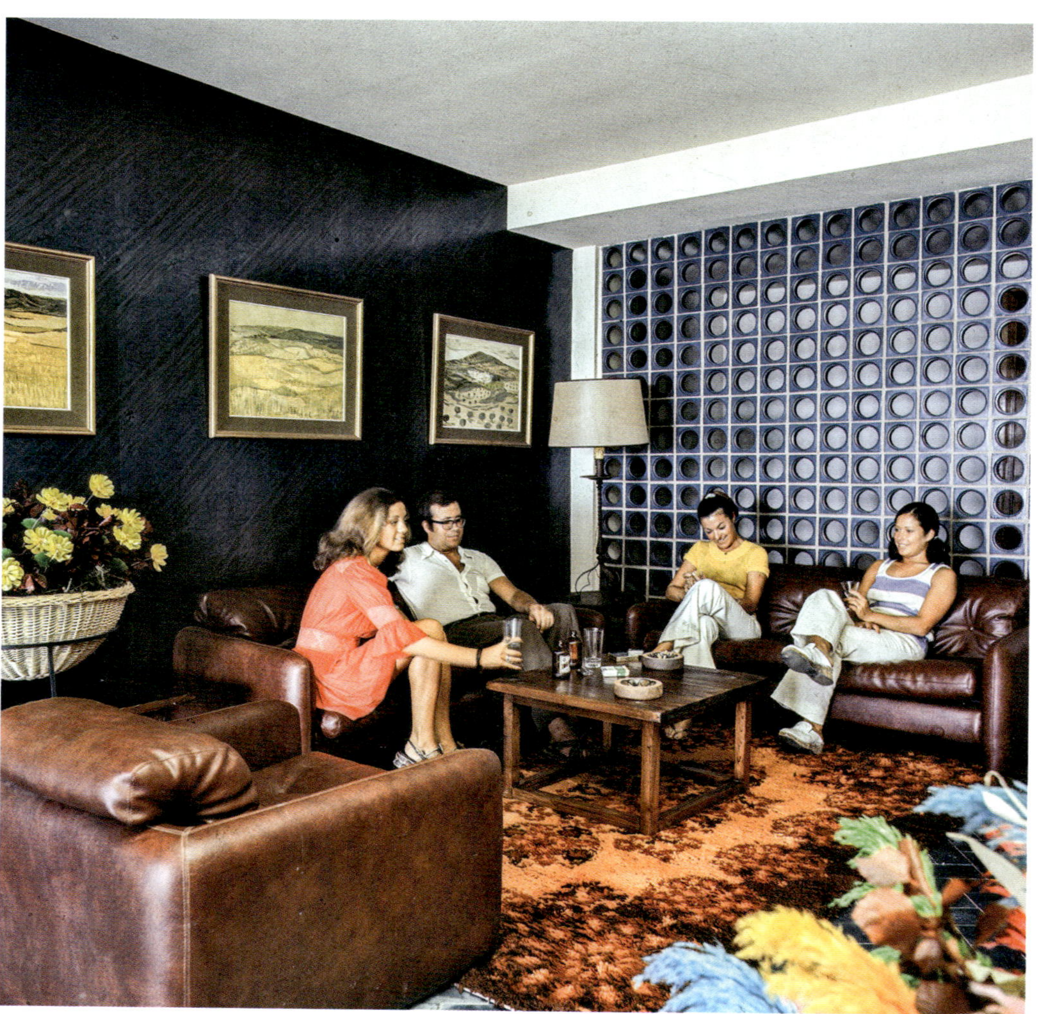

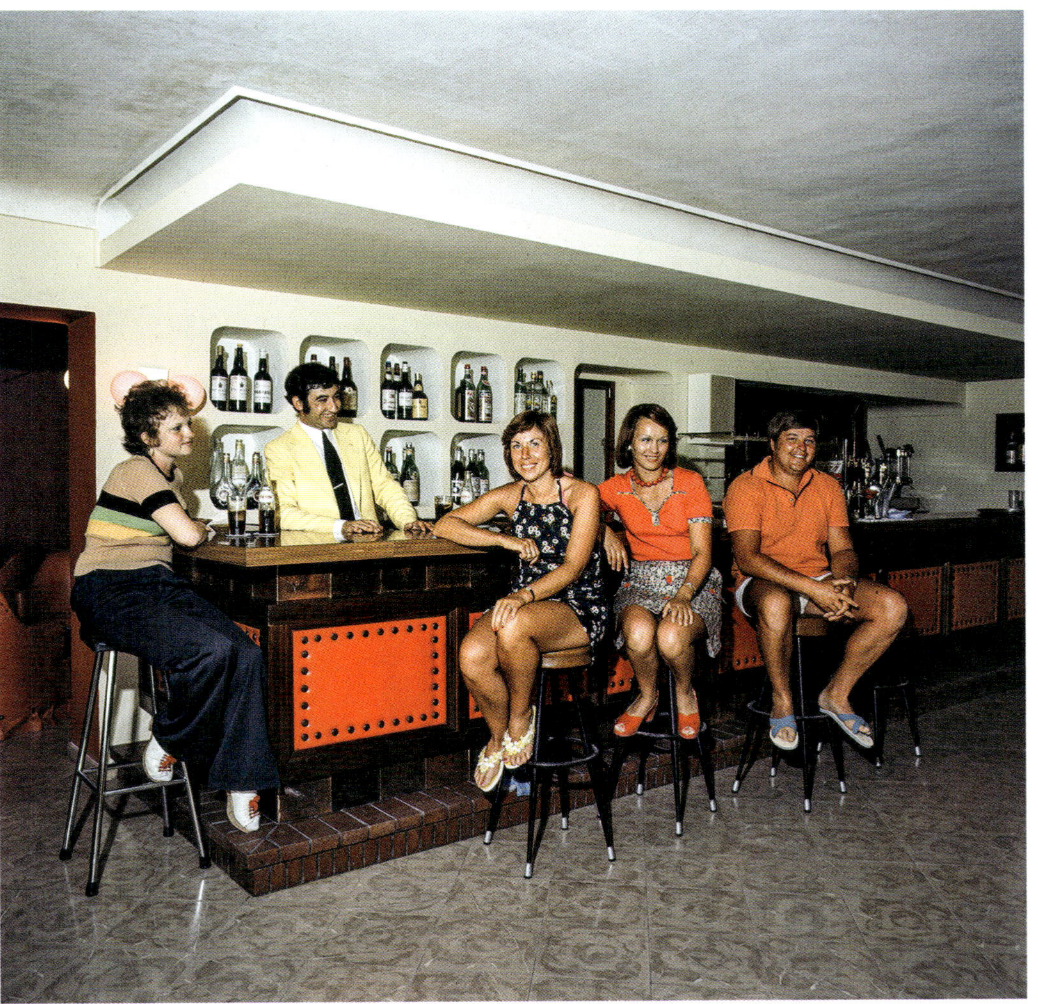

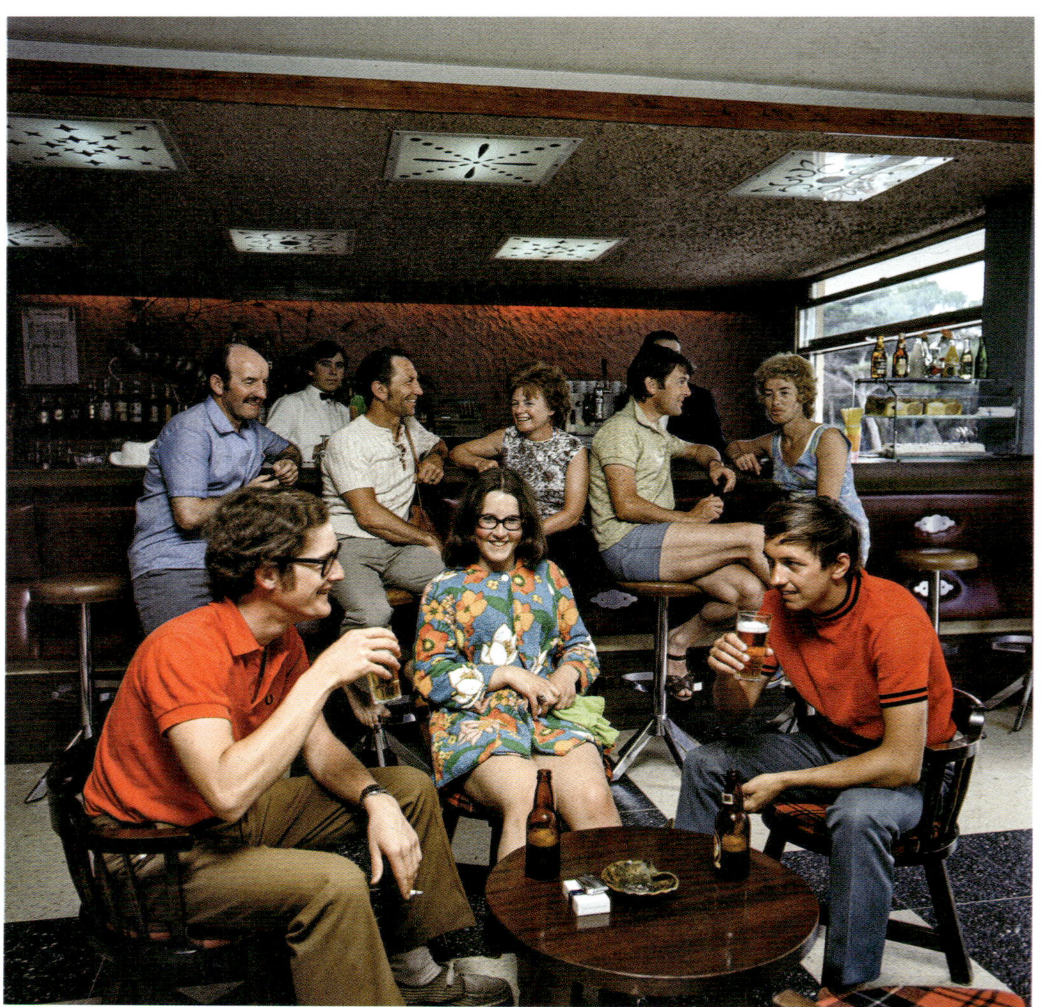

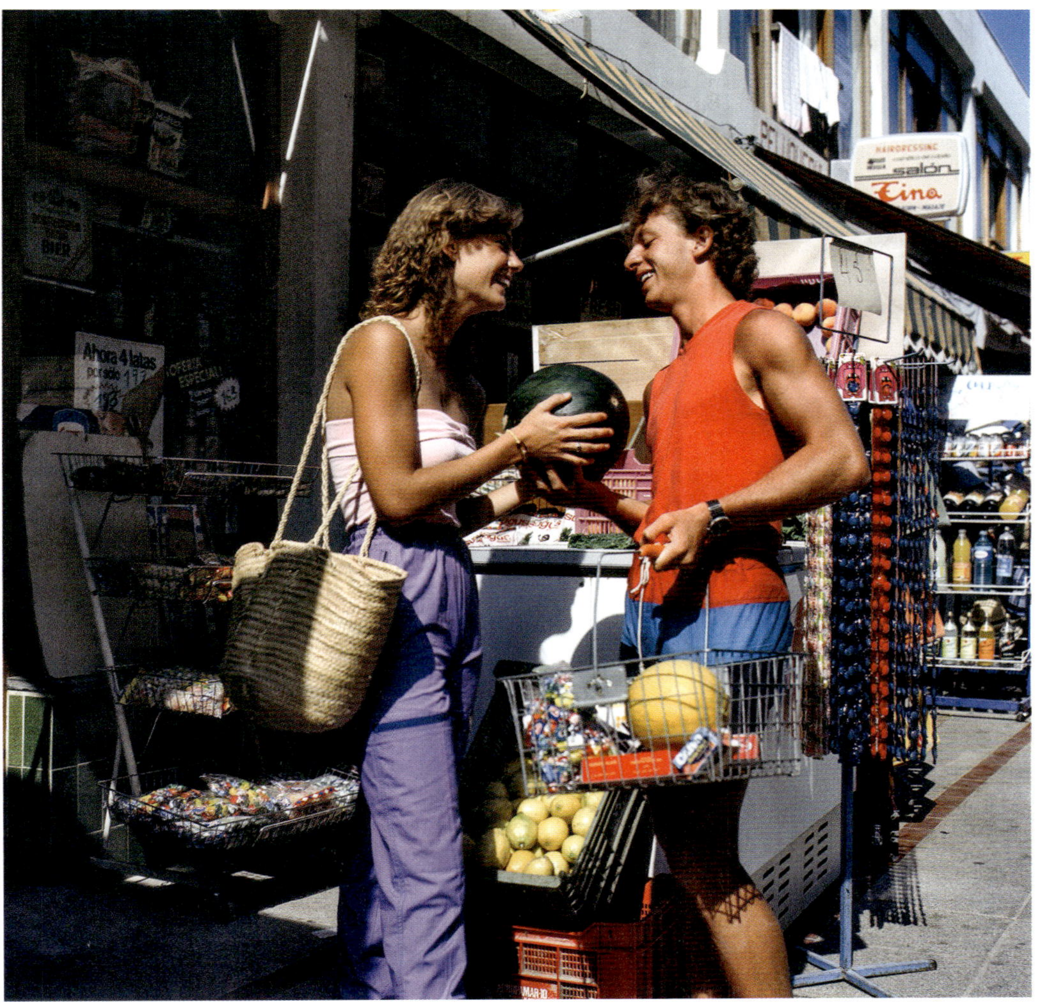

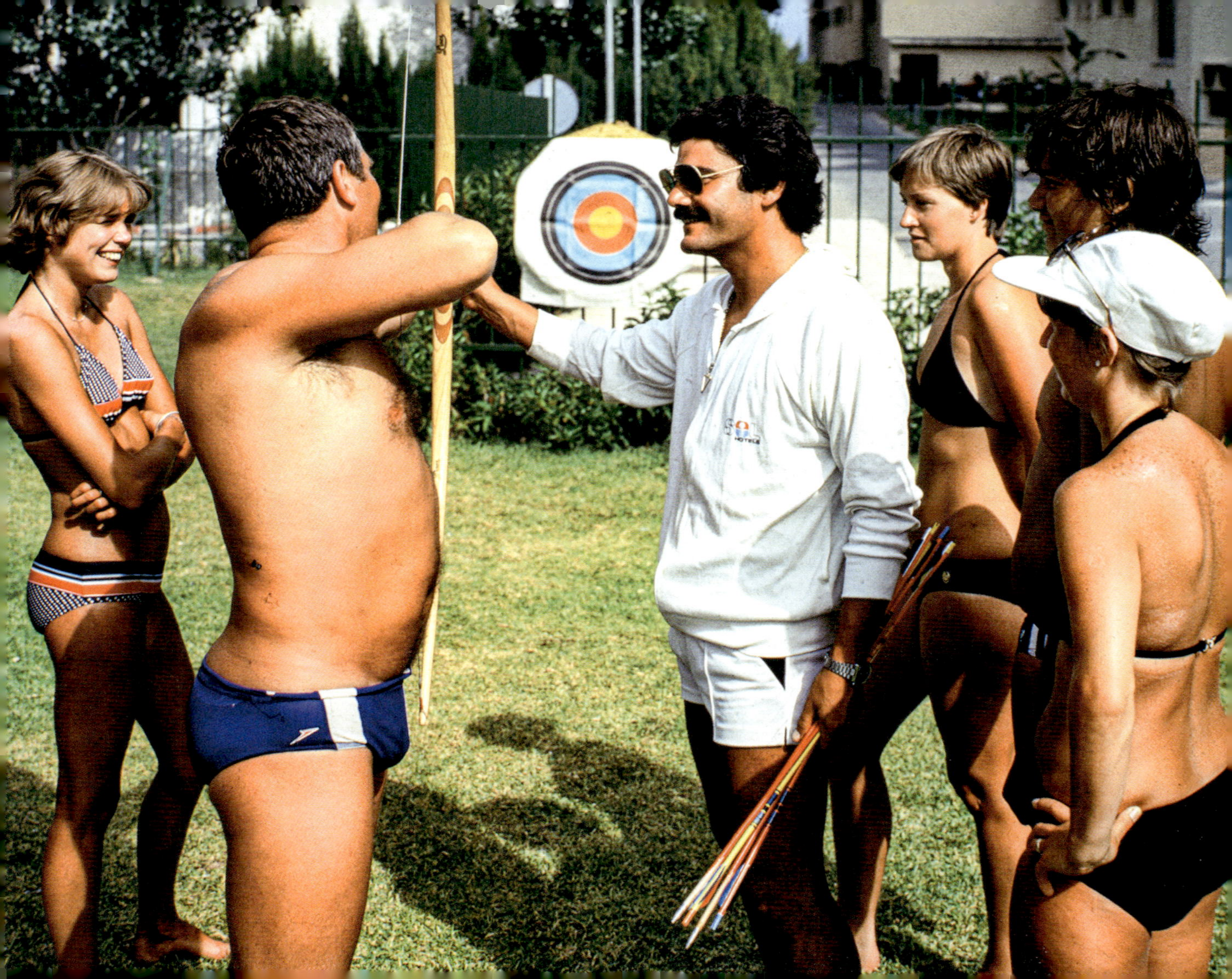

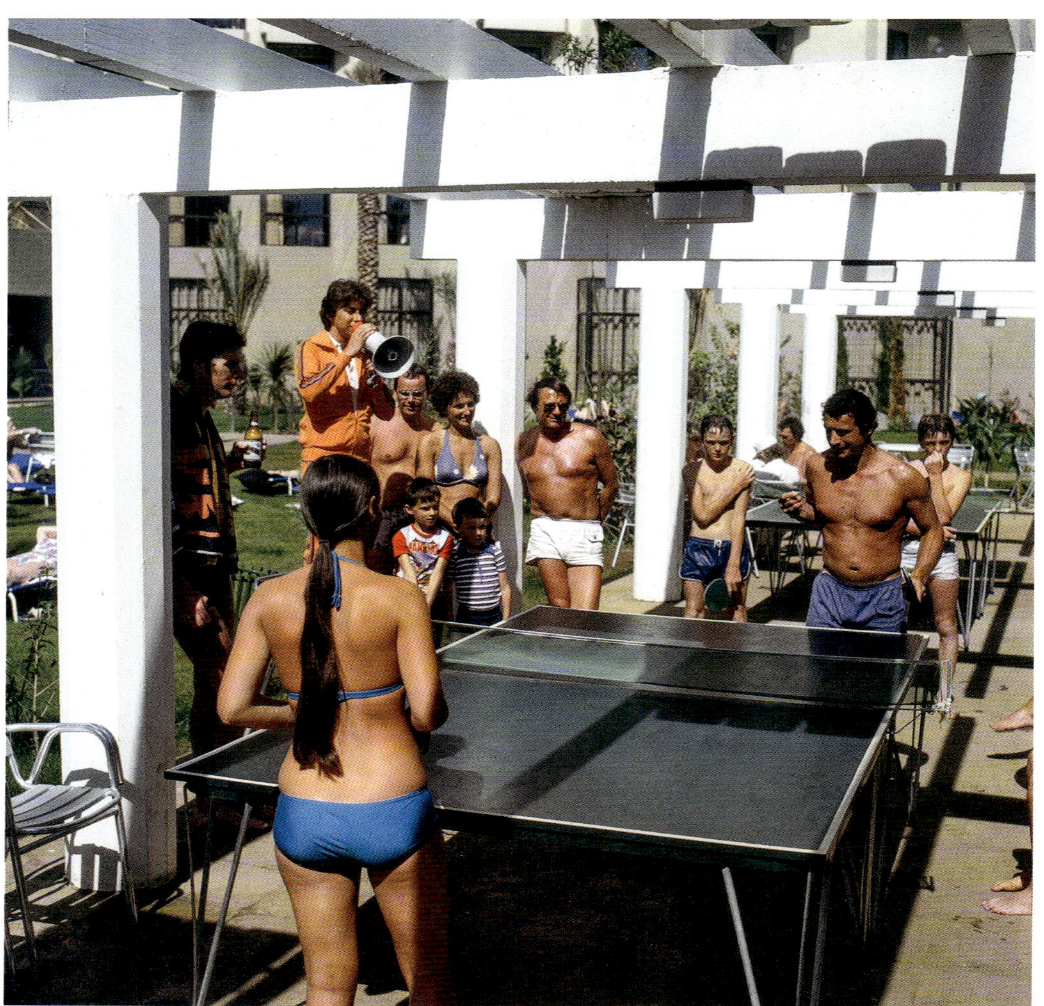

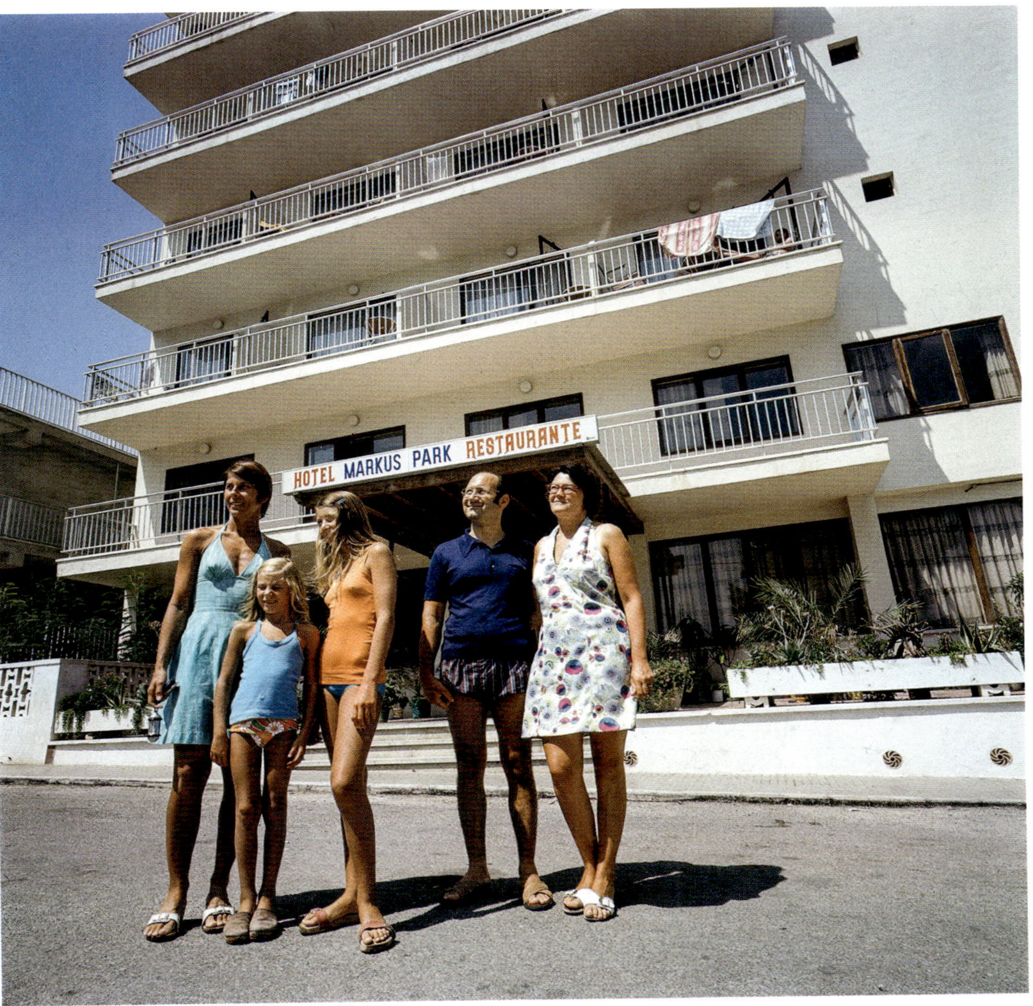

HOTEL MARKUS PARK RESTAURANTE

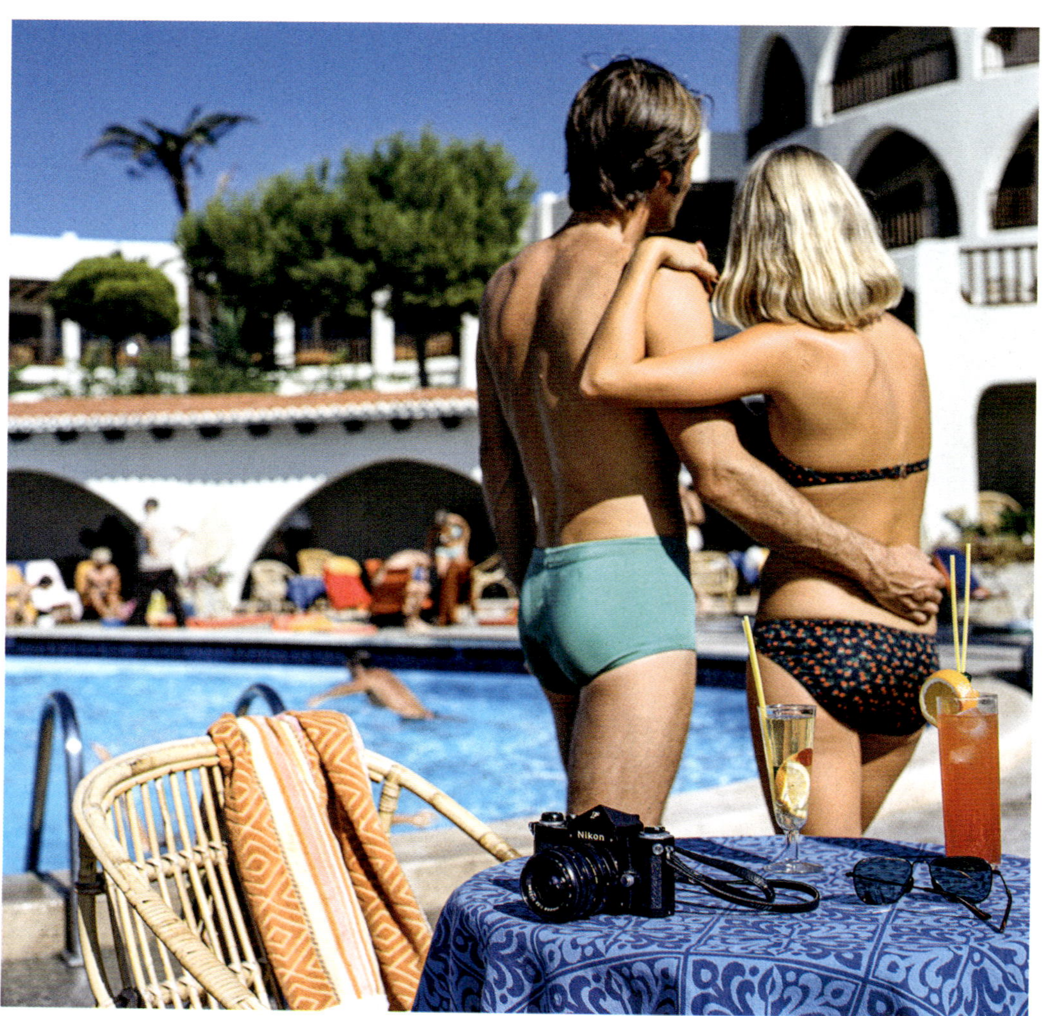

Nikon

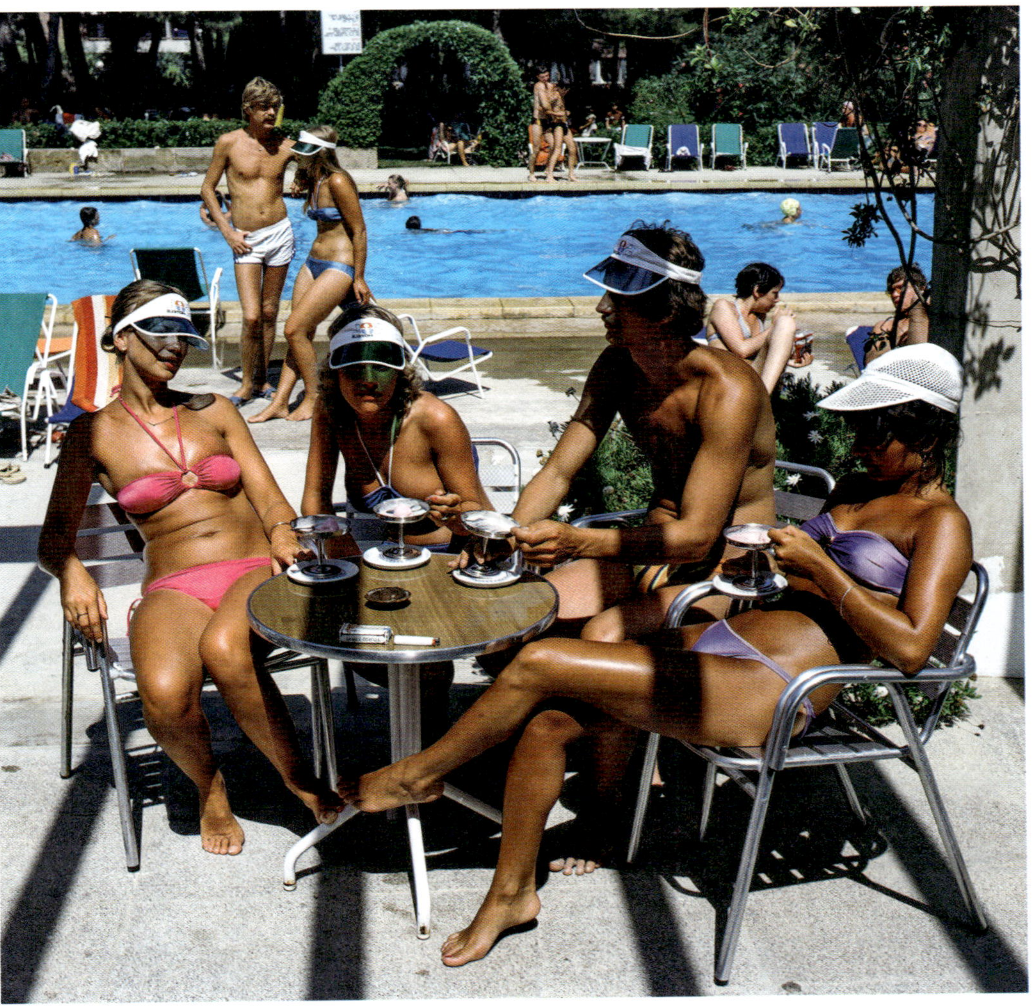

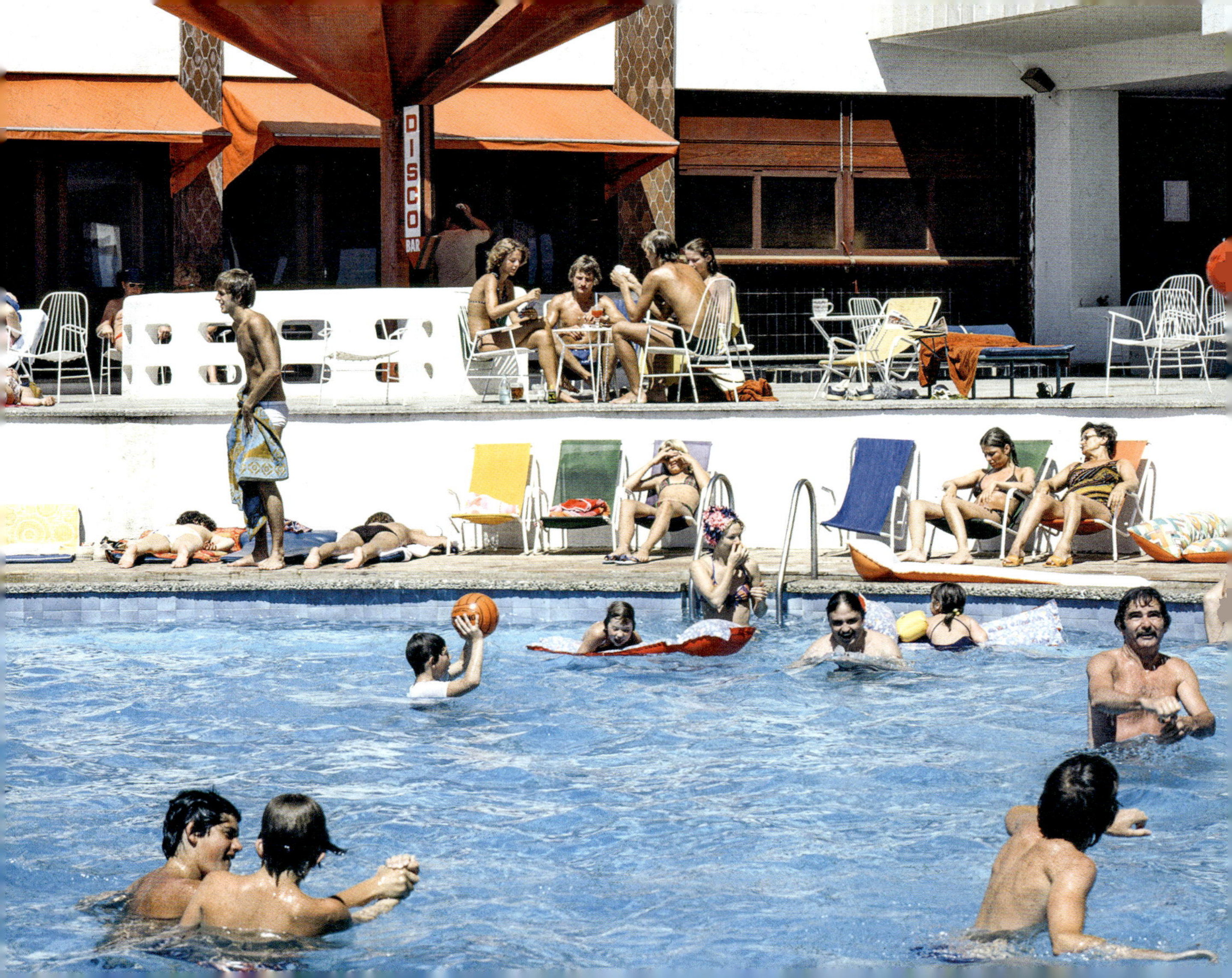
DISCO
BAR

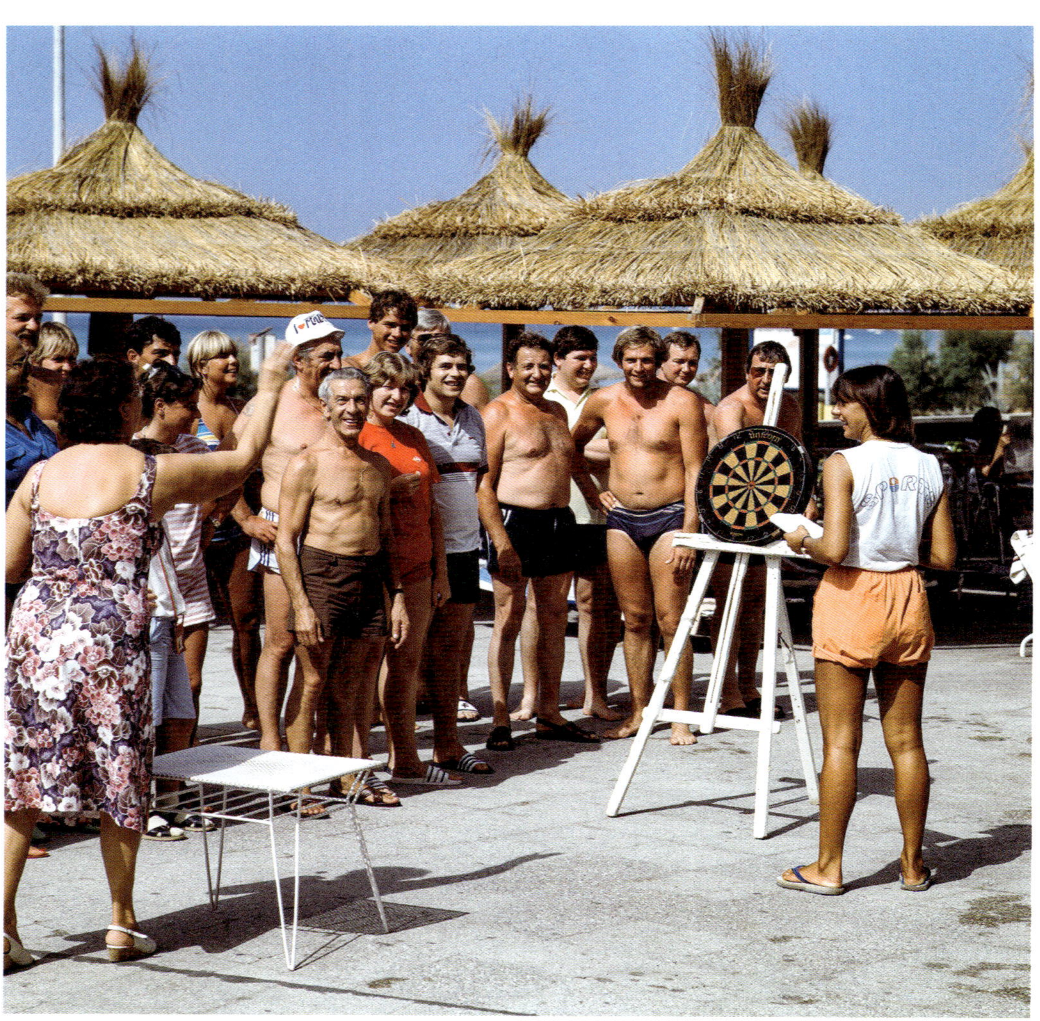

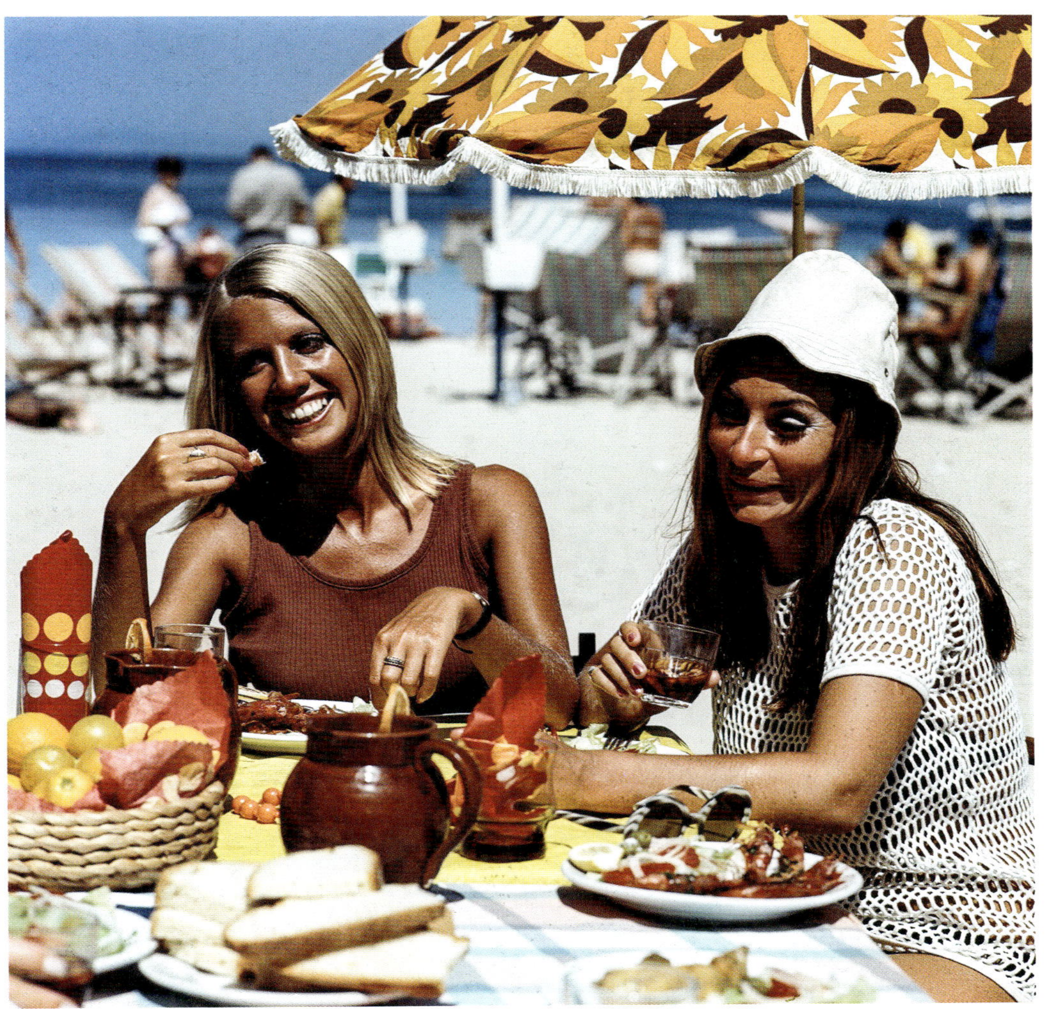

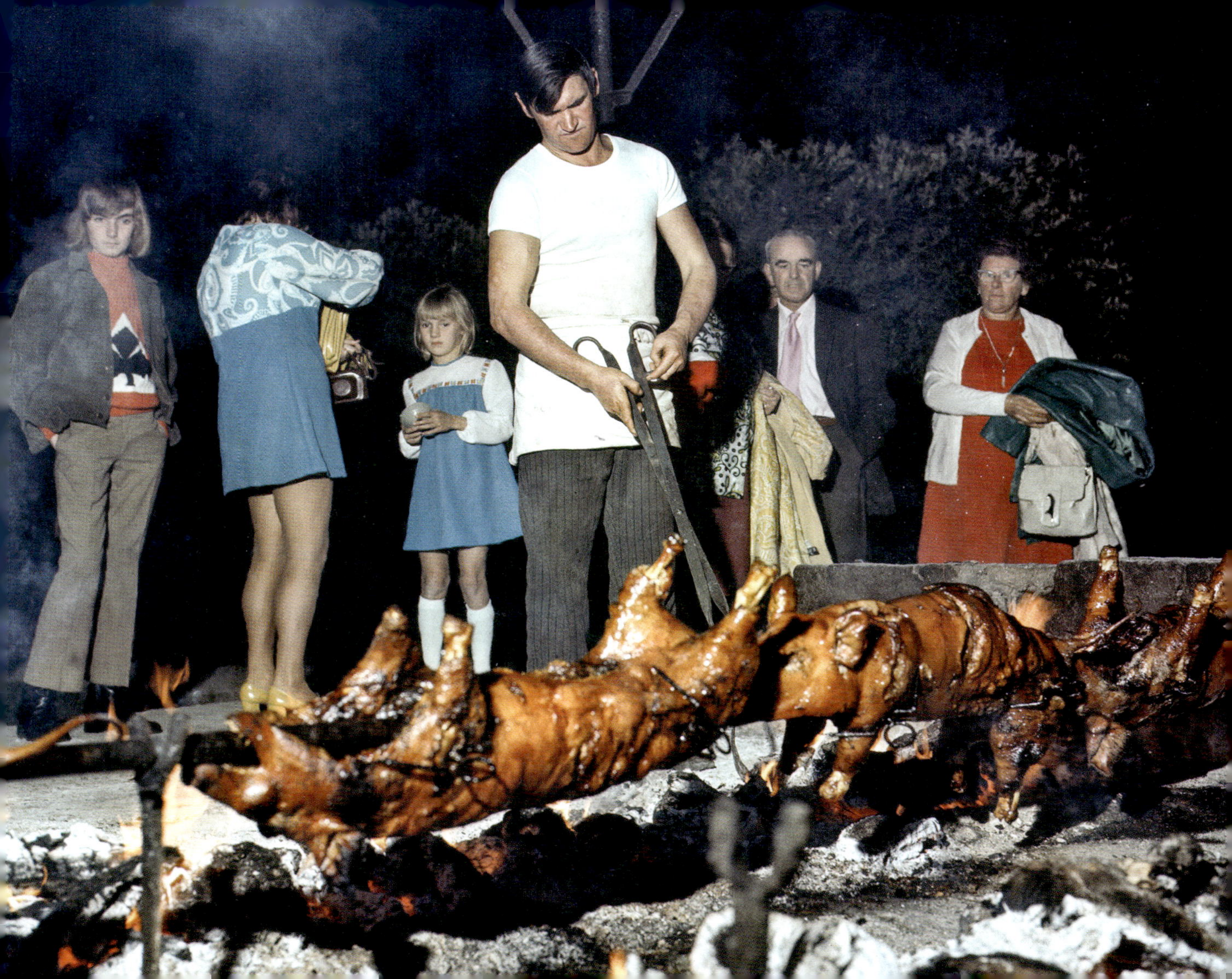

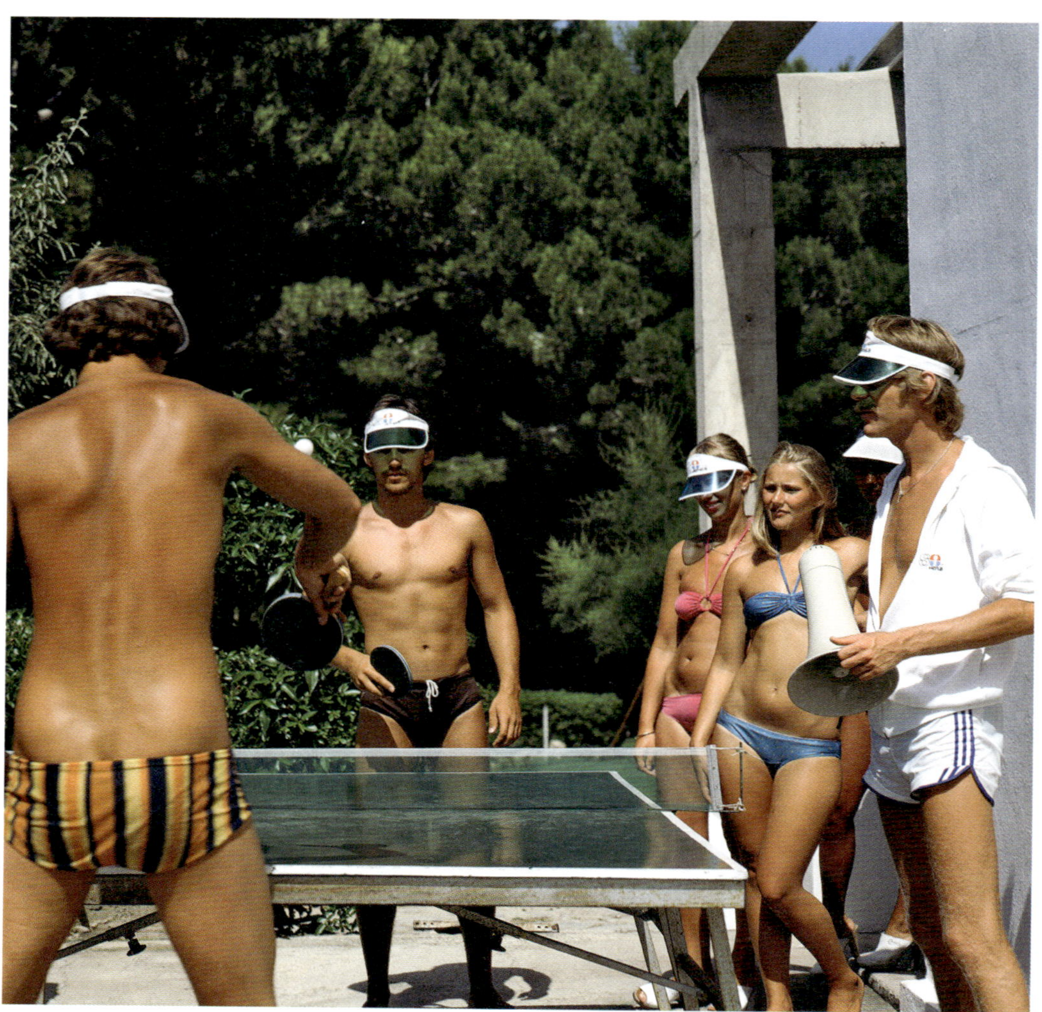

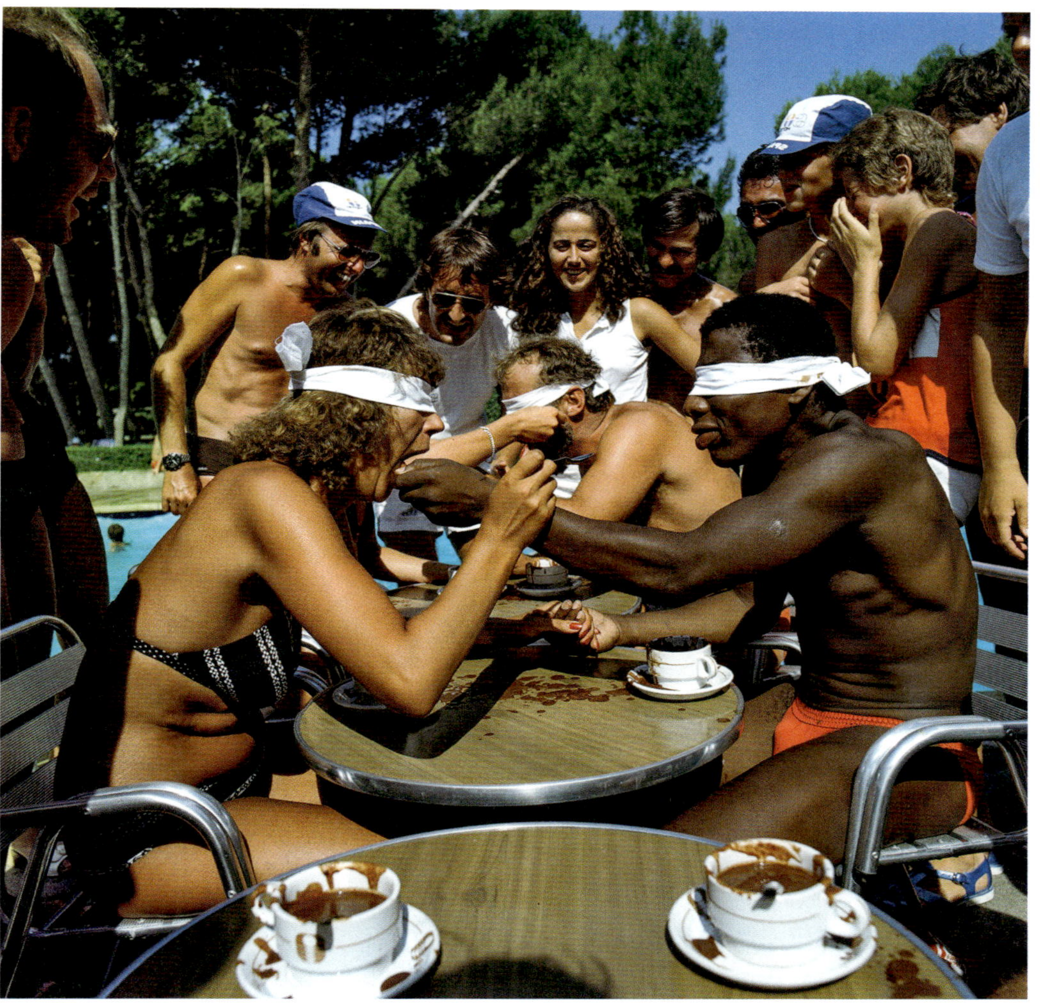

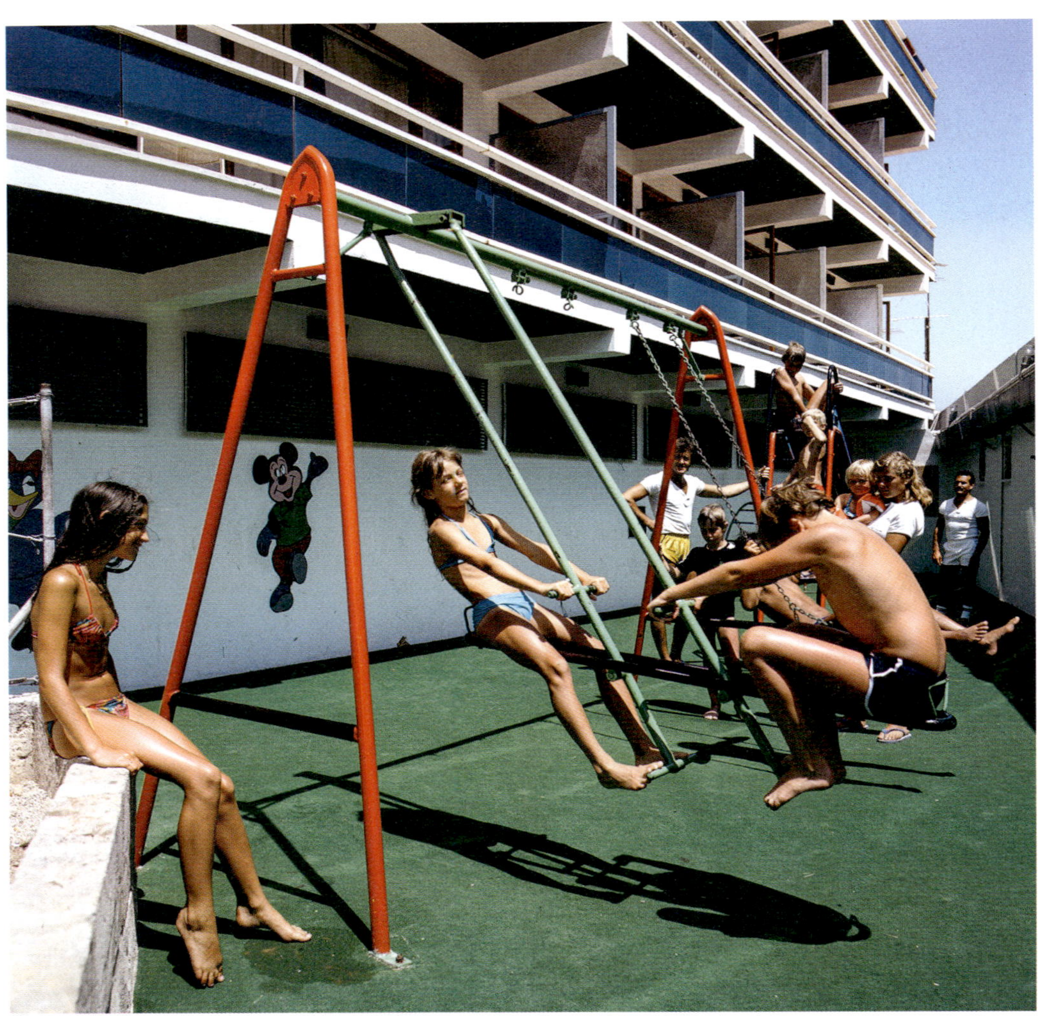

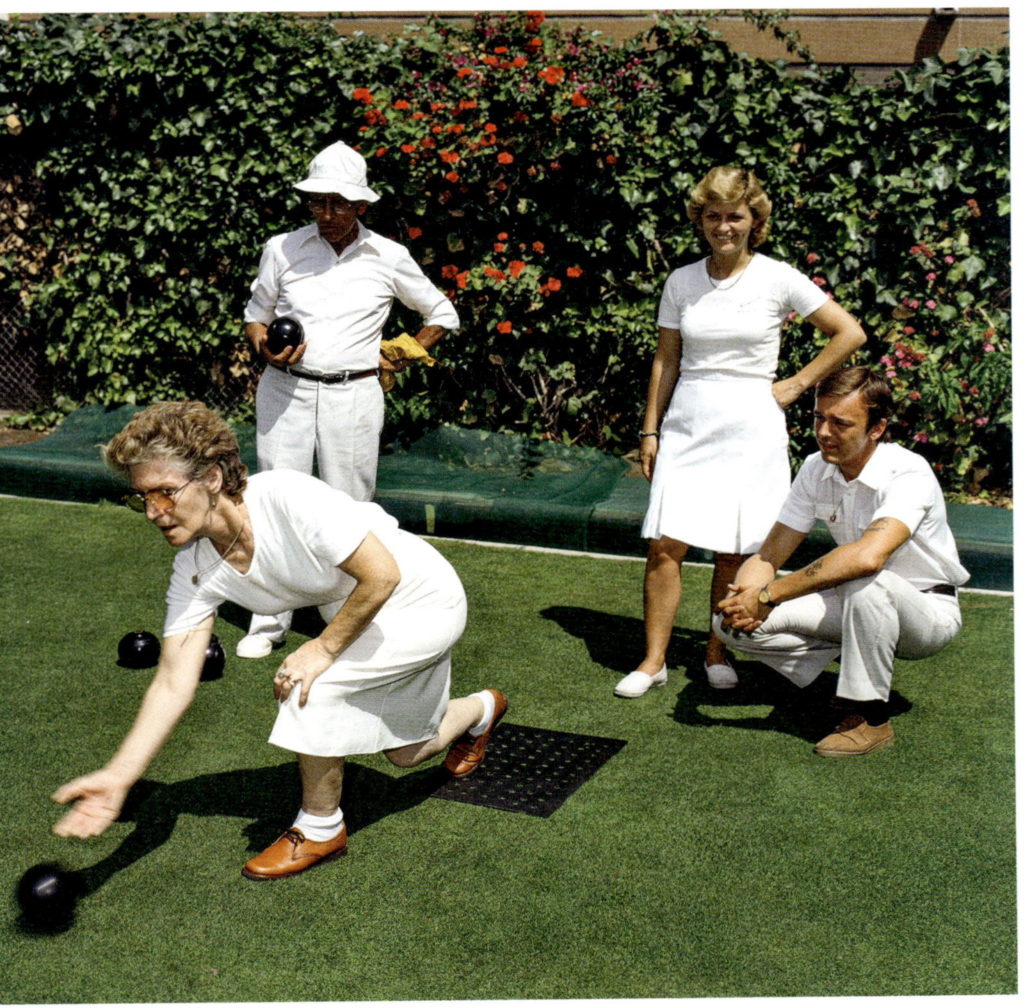

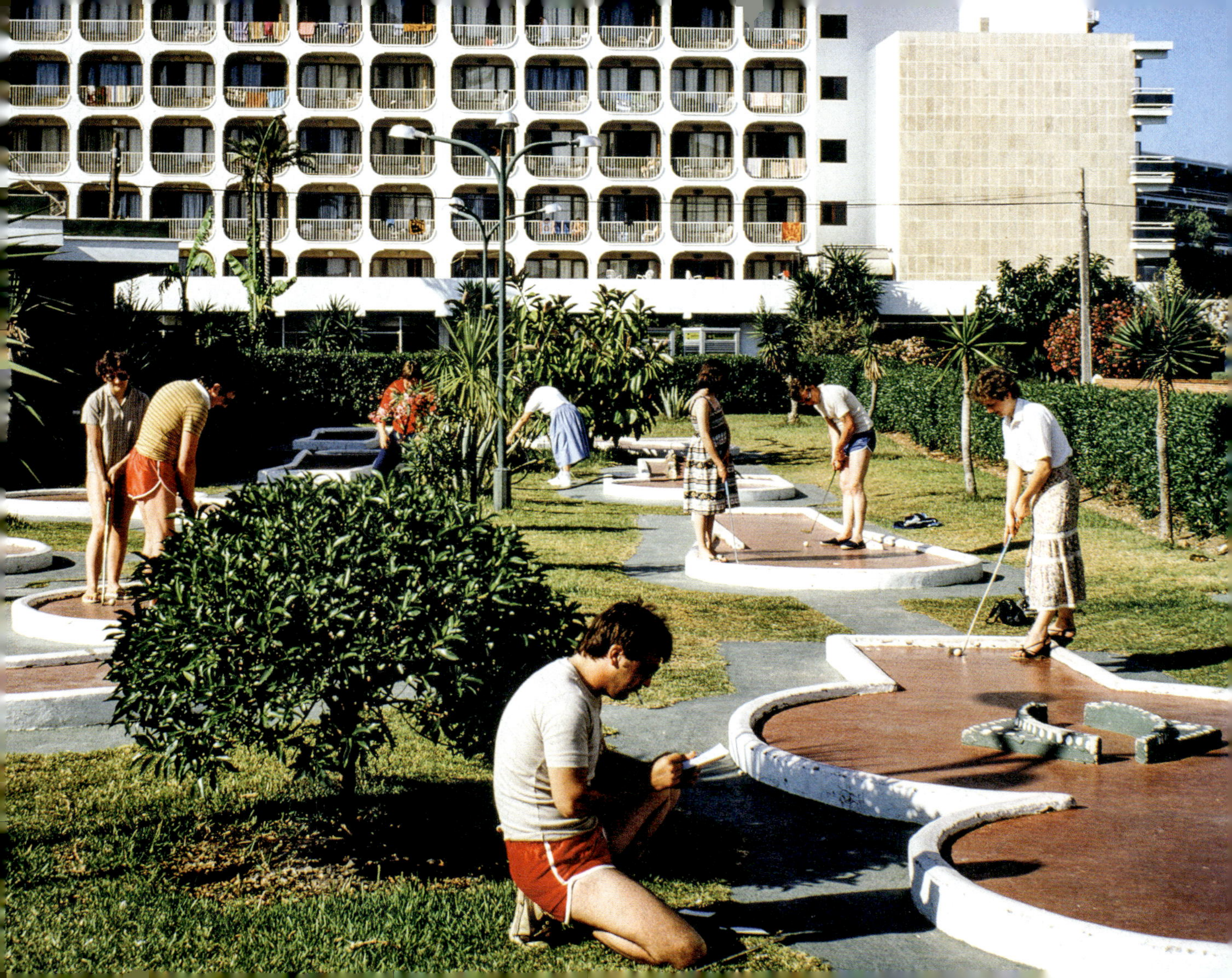

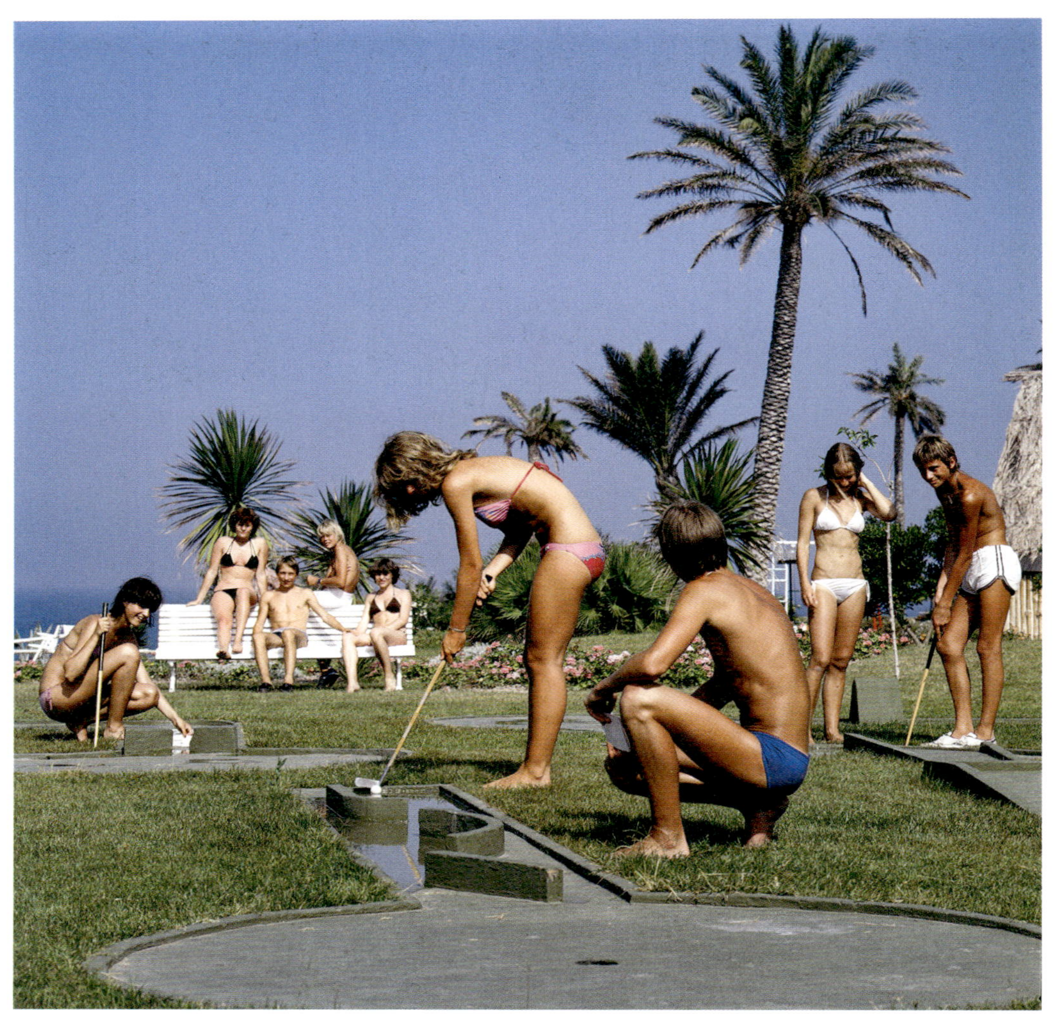

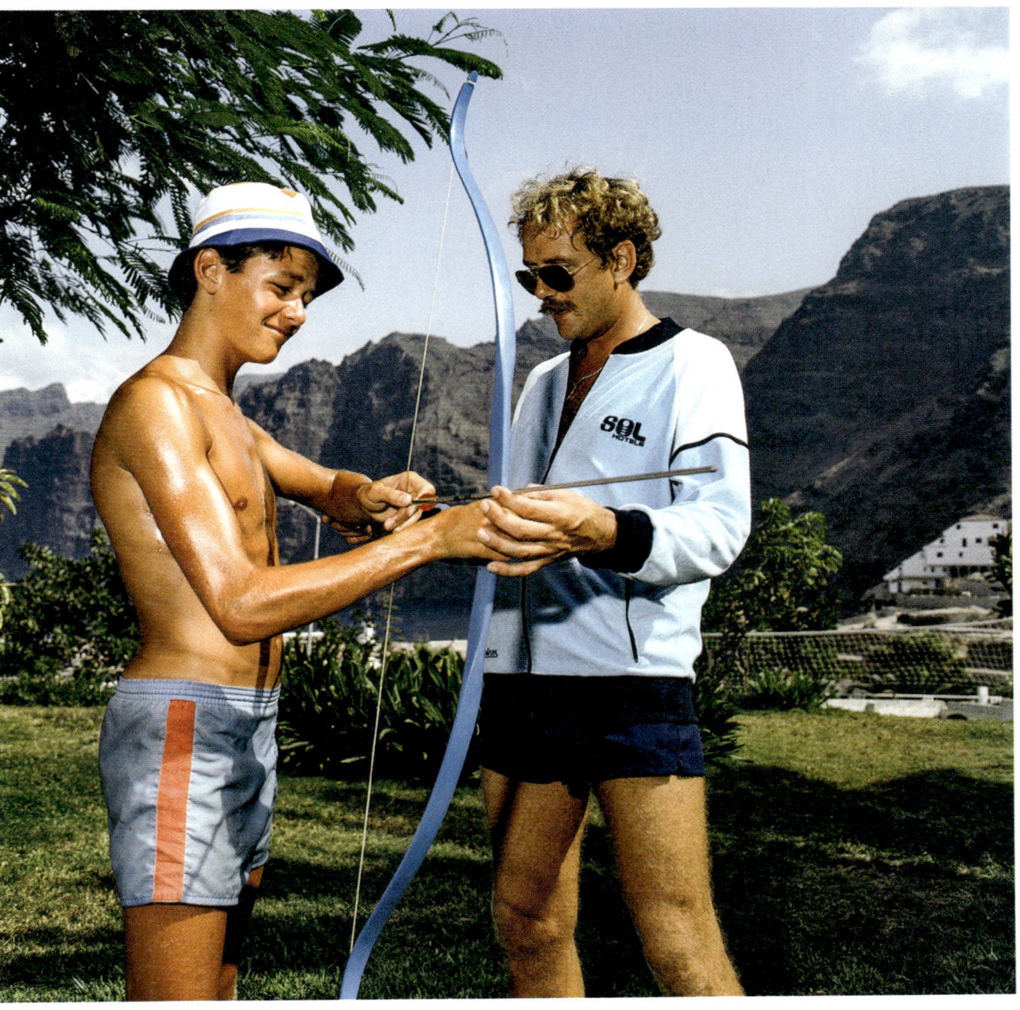

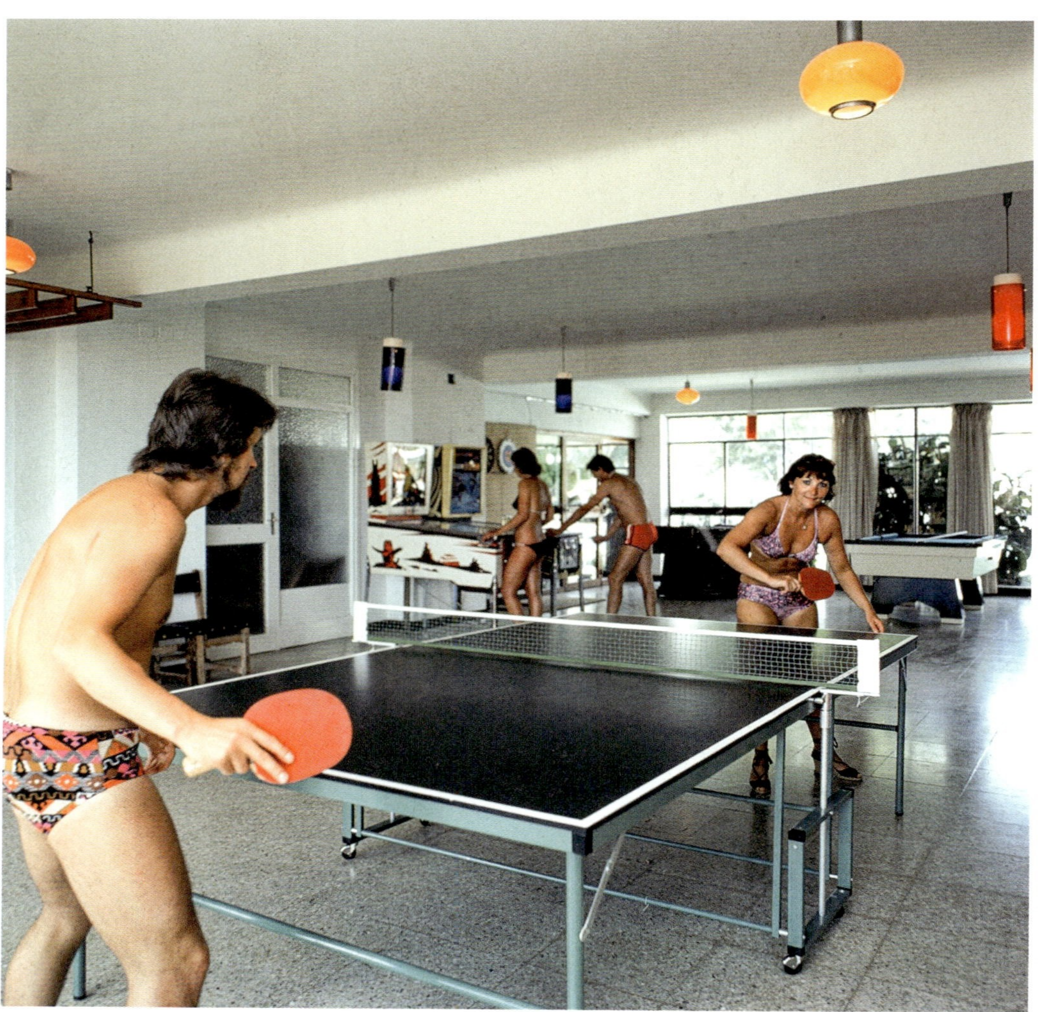

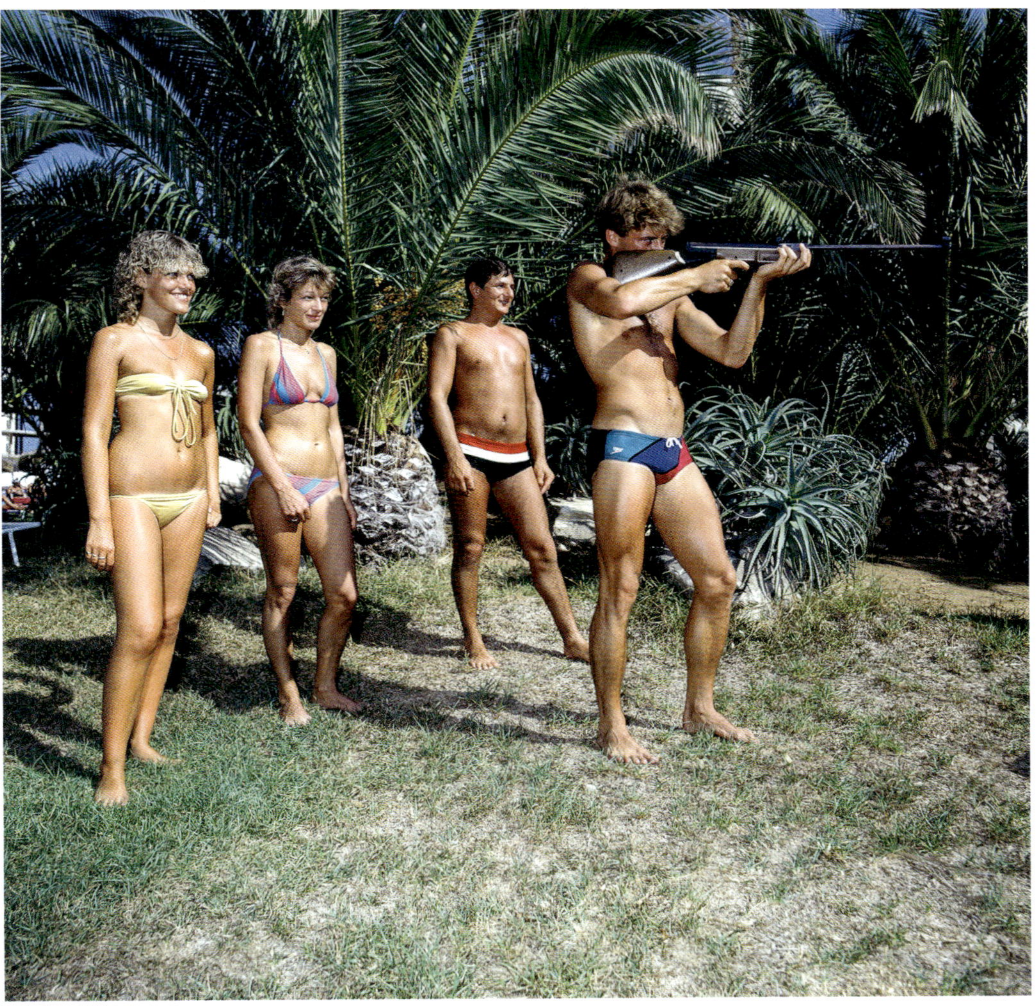

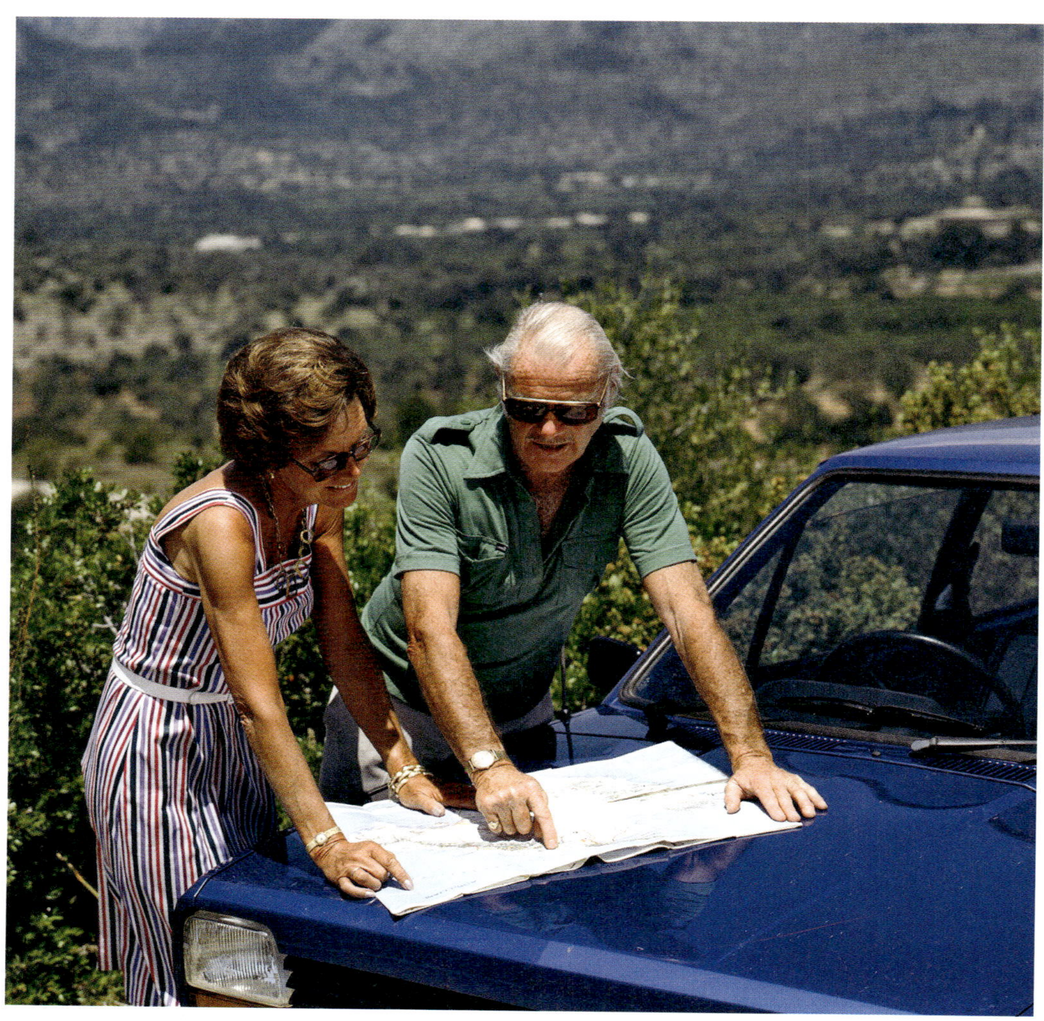

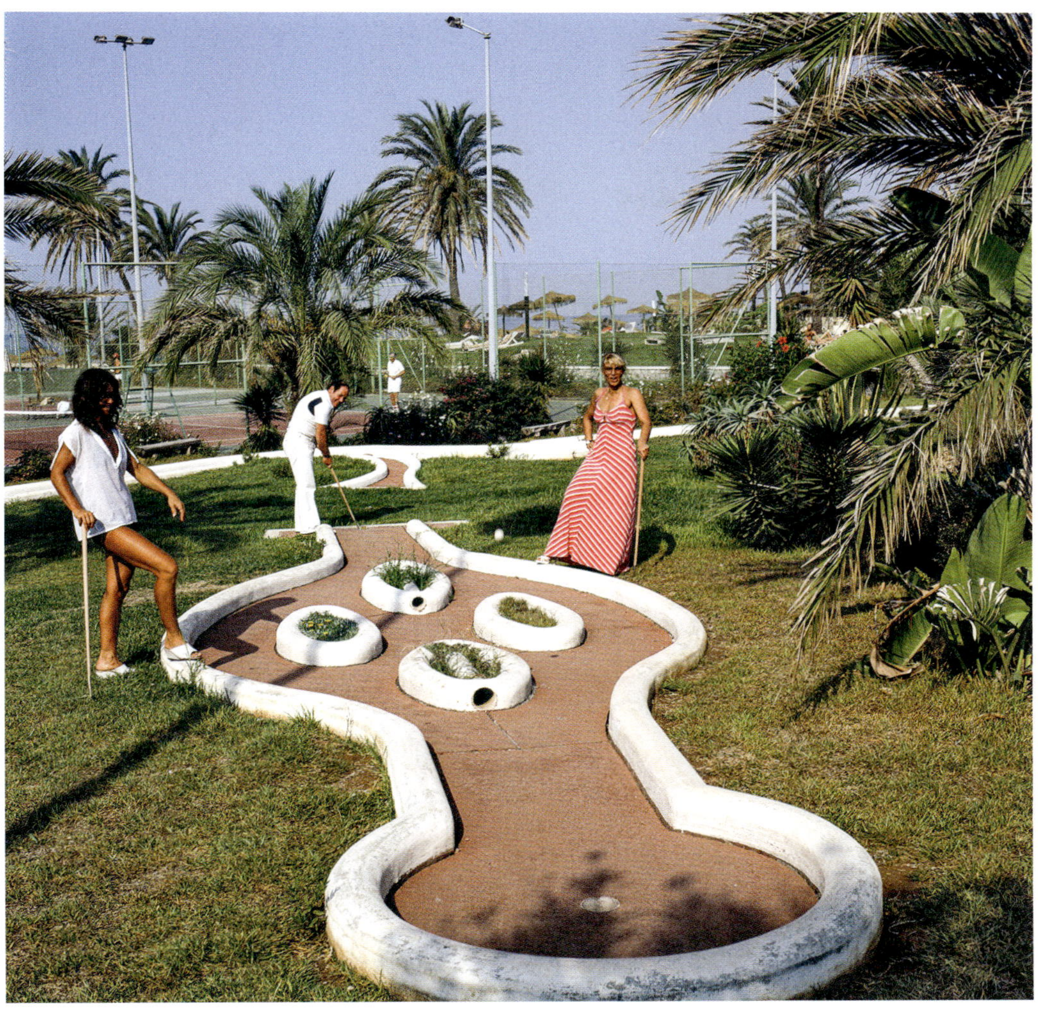

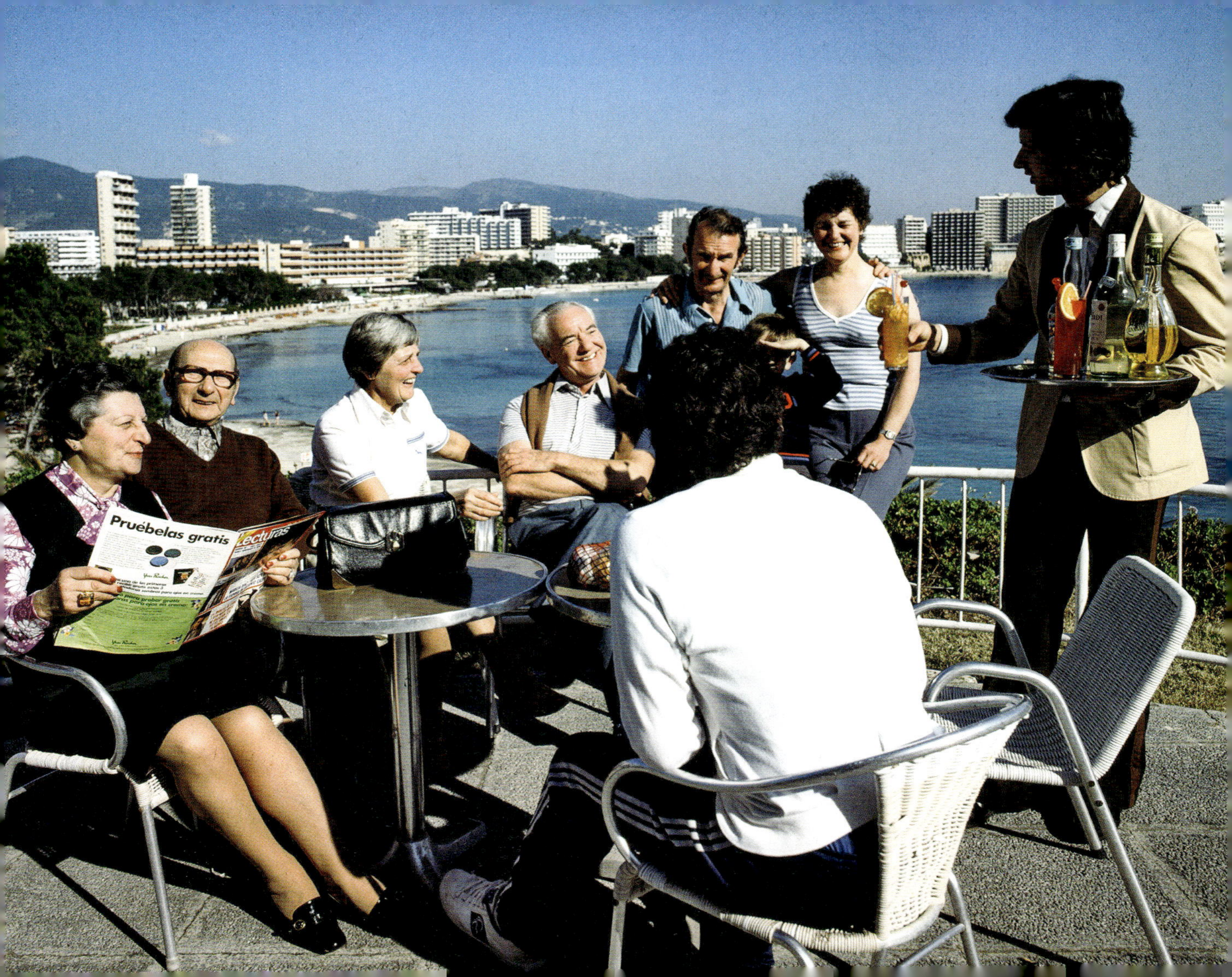
Pruébelas gratis
Yves Rocher
Lecturas

THANK YOU

Our thanks to everybody who contributed on Kickstarter

Jim Allchin
Phil Allen
Genevieve Applebee
Rebecca Applebee
Litsa Aris
Sophie Baker
David Ballantyne
Ted Barnes
Julian Barratt
Helen Barrell
Francis Barry-Walsh
Stacey Baumgarn
Andrew Beaumont
Nick Bec
Tony Benn
John Bently
Julia Biro
Duncan Blinkhorn
Polly Boccongelli
Russell Boyce

Anna Boyle
Nev Broaddragon
Kathleen Brown
Carlton Burgart
Paul Burgess
Richard Butchins
Matt Caldaralo
Martin Cameron
Arthur Cefai
Josephine Worsley Clark
D Connelly
Richard Cooper
Oliver Copeland
Tom Crispin
Nick Curtis
Catharine Denham
Ian Dickson
Uwe Diehl
Nelson Diplexcito
Jez Dobson

Peter Doig
Ina Duong
Paul Edison
Matt Edwards
Fiona Essig
Emma Faulkner
Elizabeth Fay
Matt Feeney
Tony Felgate
Grant Foster
Andrew Fowler
Molly Frances
Jason David Frost
Anna Gardiner
Bill Godber
Sera Gonzalez
Claire Greer
Louis Grey-Edwards
Christopher Gritt
Andy Hampson

John Harman
Neil Harper
Mick Harrison
Philip Hawker
Roger Healey-Dilkes
Dan Heath
Siouxsie Helliwell
Alyson Helyer
Jay Hur
Nicholas Jackson
Philip de Jersey
Lee Kearns
Ian Kinnnear
Knight of Words
Shannon LaDue
Hannah Lamb
Catherine Lawford
James Lawler
Jake Lawrence
Catherine Lette

Gideon Leventhall

Vince Lockyer

Cathy Lomax

Jane Mason

Michael McClintock

Christine McKinnon

Jeff McMillan

Martyn Miller

John Moran

David Morgan

Steven Moschidis

Mrs H and the
    Sing-Along band

Laurence Noga

Joanne Osborne

Michael Paley

Derek Palmer

Robin Panrucker

Emma Parker

Simon Parry

Gary Partington

Rebecca Pass

Stuart Pearce

Richard Pearson

Petrified Muse
    Photography

Tim Pike

Amy Pitt

Ian Pleace

Annebella Pollen

Sean Powley

Tim Pryke

Oly Ralfe

Dave Rees

Alistair Renwick

D J Roberts

Tim Roberts

Howard Rogers

Christopher Roope

Koert Schonewille

Brian Scott

Mark Sharples

Gabby Smith

Nick Smith

Warwick Smith

Becky Stacey

Oscar Stevenson

James Stewart

Paul Straghan

Caroline Streatfield

Tricia Sturn

Judyta Sufranowicz

Daryl Tebbutt

Gustav Temple

The Thorne family

Blair Todd

Zoe Trent

Covadonga Valdes

Walter Vestal

Damian Walker

David Watson

Martin Watson

Geoff Waugh

Daniel Weir

Sara Whale

Robin White

Ian Wilson

Richard Wilson

Vanessa Wilson

Josephine Wood

Eoin Woods

Christian Clark Worsley

John Wyatt-Clarke

Jay Yeomans

The Package Holiday 1968–1985

First edition, first printing, published 2024
by Hoxton Mini Press, London
Book design © Hoxton Mini Press 2024
All rights reserved

Introductions by Jan-Carlos Kucharek and Jake Clark
Copy-editing by Octavia Stocker
Proofreading by Florence Ward
Sequence by Friederike Huber
Additional design and image retouching by Richard Mason

The right of Jake Clark to be identified as the creator of this Work has
been asserted under the Copyright, Designs and Patents Act 1988.

A CIP catalogue record for this book is available from the British
Library. No part of this publication may be reproduced, stored in
a retrieval system, or transmitted in any form or by any means,
electronic, mechanical, photocopying, recording or otherwise,
without the prior written permission of the copyright owner.

ISBN: 978-1-914314-58-2

Printed and bound by OZGraf, Poland

Hoxton Mini Press is an environmentally conscious publisher,
committed to offsetting our carbon footprint. The offset for this book
was purchased from Stand For Trees.

For every order you place on our website, we plant a tree:
www.hoxtonminipress.com

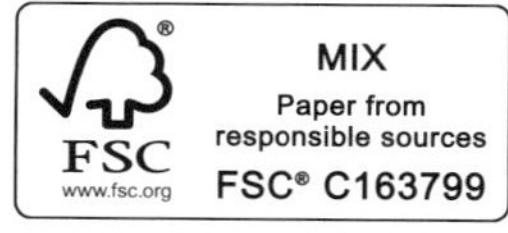